Maureen Dunbar

Catherine

The Story of a Young Girl
Who Died of Anorexia

VIKING

VIKING

Penguin Books Ltd, Harmondsworth, Middlesex, England
Viking Penguin Inc., 40 West 23rd Street, New York, New York 10010, U.S.A.
Penguin Books Australia Ltd, Ringwood, Victoria, Australia
Penguin Books Canada Limited, 2801 John Street, Markham, Ontario, Canada L3R 1B4
Penguin Books (N.Z.) Ltd, 182–190 Wairau Road, Auckland 10, New Zealand

First published 1986
Copyright © Maureen Dunbar, 1986

Printed in Great Britain by
Richard Clay (The Chaucer Press) Ltd,
Bungay, Suffolk
Filmset in 11/14pt Monophoto Photina by
Northumberland Press Ltd, Gateshead,
Tyne and Wear

British Library Cataloguing in Publication Data
Dunbar, Maureen
    Catherine.
    1. Anorexia nervosa—Patients—Biography
    I. Title
    616.85'2   RC552.A5

ISBN 0–670–81014–2

*This book is our testimony to you, dearest Catherine;
we love you, we miss you*

Mummy, Daddy, Simon, Richard and Anna

ACKNOWLEDGEMENTS

So many friends by their love, support and acts of kindness, to Catherine and to us, helped to give us the strength to cope both with Catherine's illness and afterwards with the grief of her loss. We would specially like to mention Mary and Duncan Nicholson, Terry Helson, Joëlle Jeffries, Sister Marie McLoughlin, Dr Margaret Foot, Anne Fryer, Barbara Dewar, Katie Hughes, Father Patrick Taggart, Father John Watts and many, many others.

Our love and gratitude to you all,
The Dunbar Family

ONE

My daughter, Catherine Ann Marie, died of anorexia nervosa on 2 January 1984, at the age of twenty-two. She was intelligent, sensitive and beautiful, but she only wanted to die.

With hindsight, I think Catherine believed that I accepted her anorexia or, to put it differently, I accepted her own denial of the will to live. I never did; what I did understand, and understood very well, was that this was her *anorexia* controlling her and not *her* herself. I constantly tried to explain this to family and friends. To express my deepest feelings about Catherine's illness is impossible. Words fail me. Uppermost in my mind was always the urgent need to infuse in her the desire to live – and I failed.

I was always aware of this unspoken conflict between Catherine and myself, the conflict of her wanting to die and me wanting her to live, and now I wonder whether she felt that too. It used to stir up all the pain I could not show her, but at the very end the most important thing to me was that, whether she lived or died, she was happy. I believe she achieved much of this happiness in the last weeks of her life and complete happiness in those last precious days. She no longer asked, 'When will I die, when will God take me?' I feel certain now that when she was close to dying she *was* living in the present and not longing for death any more. Catherine, a girl who from a small child had always had a deep faith, was at last able to grasp the meaning of peace in Christ, that his loving arms were holding her *there* and *then*, that she was protecting her family by her love and prayers *there* and *then*. She no longer kept asking the question, 'When will God take me?' because she knew instinctively that her heaven had already started. Marie, a dear friend and past teacher of Catherine's, wrote to her, 'Do not forget that the present moment is nearer to eternity than the past or future; we almost touch eternity when we live in the present'; I believe she finally understood and felt the truth and wonder of these words.

I feel her loss so deeply, her loss as a beautiful daughter, her loss as a sister to Simon, Richard and Anna, the loss of children she would have had, my grandchildren, the loss of her as a person who could have done and given so much. I hope I showed her and told her how much I loved her often enough. I know she understood and forgave me for the times I was irritable, impatient and tired, sometimes so tired that I didn't want to know about her illness. Not until we lose someone do we understand the depth of our love.

I hope I can be a better person for having known Catherine, loved her and suffered with her. I thank God for my faith, for without it I would not have had the strength and endurance to cope. After she died I too wished to die, for several days I carried this deep desire to die within me. It gave me peace and at times a feeling of great happiness. But despite my overriding feelings of devastation and loneliness, and an infinite sadness, I realized that I had much to do, much to live for, and that life for me had to go on. Catherine and I underwent much pain and anguish together, but we enjoyed much that was good too.

My hope was always that Catherine would overcome her anorexia and so, with her special knowledge, be able to help others, but she was trapped, trapped in a maze of agony and delusions. She suffered too intolerance and lack of understanding in others; I hope that this book will help to create a climate of compassion, love and support from the families and friends of those unfortunate enough to be anorectic.

TWO

One weekday in January 1977, Catherine's boarding-school headmistress rang me to tell me that she was worried because Catherine did not appear to be eating anything. My feeling was that she might not be eating the school meals, but was most probably living on food I had given her from home. The following Saturday the headmistress telephoned me again and said that she would be arranging for a member of staff to drive Catherine and her sister Anna to the station as she was so concerned for Catherine. I met them as usual off the train and the feeling of shock I felt at seeing Catherine is as vivid today as it was then. She was pale, drawn and hollow-eyed, and able to walk only very slowly. We took a taxi home from Victoria. When we arrived, my son Simon was on the doorstep with a school friend; for a moment he failed to recognize Catherine; he thought she must be one of her friends. It should have been a happy day, for that morning Simon had heard he had been given a place the following October at his first choice of medical school.

Catherine was then fifteen years old and this marked the beginning of my realization that something was seriously wrong with her. She had always been a difficult eater – I suppose the problem started when I decided to bottle-feed her at about eight weeks old. Simon was two and a half and Richard sixteen months when Catherine was born. Life was hectic and exhausting looking after three very young children, so it was not surprising that my milk supply began to decrease. For a time bottle-feeding proved disastrous. Nothing suited Kate. ('Kate' was easier for Simon and Richard to pronounce.) I tried every brand of baby food on the market; I tried diluted cow's milk; no one suggested I tried goat's milk and I did not think of it myself. Her abdomen would become swollen and hard; she would bring up a great deal of wind and was obviously in pain. When she suffered these bouts the only way I could give her relief was to lay her on her tummy across my lap and gently rub her back. Eventually, our family doctor sought the advice of a paediatrician. He suggested I cut out all milk and give her Ribena to drink and Farex mixed with water. She thrived on this. He told me that if she had an allergy to milk then she would never be able to tolerate it, but when she was about two I discovered her sharing her brothers' ice-cream with no ill effects, and from then on I gradually added milk to her diet. (She adored milk puddings.) Nevertheless, she was a problem child when it came to eating; whereas Simon and Richard – and later her sister Anna – would eat almost anything and everything with obvious enjoyment, Kate was extremely finicky. She would refuse to eat meat, fish, eggs and vegetables. For years her diet consisted of bread, butter, peanut butter, milk puddings, a little cheese, yoghurt, fruit and occasionally a sausage or rasher of bacon. Remembering the miseries I had endured as a child of being forced to eat what I didn't like, I never forced Kate. She was very healthy, so was obviously getting sufficient nutriment. Apart from the usual childhood illnesses she was never ill and rarely caught a cold. My husband John's attitude, however, was different – he believed that children should eat what was prepared for the family and he would make no exception for Kate. This meant that meals at the weekend were a problem for her and I would frequently remove her plate when he wasn't looking. I remember one occasion when Kate was staying for a few days with my sister Eileen and her family; she was just three years old at the time. Eileen was at her wits' end because Kate just wasn't eating anything. One morning while they were out shopping Kate pointed to some sausage rolls. Eileen rushed in and bought half a dozen. On arriving home she sat Kate down and gave her a sausage roll, feeling great relief that at last Kate was going to eat something. She did, but she first painstakingly removed every bit of sausage meat before proceeding to eat the pastry!

It was at this time that I had become concerned about Kate's speech. It was very indistinct, and only her close family could understand her. Her brothers, on the other hand, had learned to talk clearly at an early age, and both had had a reasonable vocabulary by the age of two and a half. Kate at three and a half seemed, in this respect, much slower. She was also very nervous of people and would rarely reply when spoken to. Anna, the youngest, was now six months old and on one of our routine visits to the doctor for Anna's vaccination, I mentioned Kate's slowness in talking. I was ticked off for comparing her with her brothers and told it was probably due to catarrh! I knew very well that I shouldn't compare my children, that each child is an individual and develops in his or her own good time, but I suspected that something could be preventing the normal development in talking in Kate's case. I vividly remember one incident some weeks after our visit to the doctor. Kate, who loved to help me with the household chores, was 'helping' me to make the beds. She asked me a question (I can't remember what it was). I replied. She went on to ask the same question three or four times. I replied with the same answer, gradually getting more impatient. I stopped what I was doing and said crossly, 'Kate, why do you keep asking the same question? I have told you the answer.' As I was saying this it dawned on me that Kate might be deaf; perhaps she could only understand me when she could see my lips. At that moment everything became clear – while making the bed my head had been down and she couldn't see my lip movements. When reading her stories I would sit her on my lap and she would always put her hand under my chin; I now realized why – it was so that she could lipread.

Within a week I had an appointment for Kate with an audiologist who confirmed that Kate had a considerable hearing loss. Within another week we were seeing the consultant at the local hospital. He gave her more tests and told me he was impressed by the level of her understanding in view of her handicap. Her hearing loss was due to enlarged adenoids. At the age of four she was admitted into hospital and the adenoids removed. I bought her a pretty new dressing-gown for the occasion and washed the old cot blanket which she always liked to have with her. (She called it her 'night-night'.) She would rub the edge of this, which was still bound with satin, though somewhat frayed, across her upper lip before going to sleep. All went well until the moment I had to leave; then she clung to me sobbing and screaming. Tears were streaming down my face too – I couldn't bear to leave her. There were no facilities for mothers to stay with their children and visiting was strictly limited to the set times. Eventually, I was able to leave when I assured her I would be staying upstairs in the 'Mummies' Ward'. Next day I rang to find out how she was after the operation. I was told it would be better not to see her until the following day. Knowing she would be distraught if I wasn't there when she came round from the anaesthetic I went to the hospital, but the sister-in-charge of the ward refused to allow me to see Kate, saying that she was sleeping peacefully. Feeling unhappy, I returned home, consoling myself with the thought that perhaps they did know best. The following day I learned from one of the other mothers that Kate had cried her heart out for me and had been refused her 'night-night' – despite her telling the sister that Mummy had washed it! How much more enlightened attitudes are today with regard to children in hospital.

Once home her speech developed rapidly and she gradually gained in confidence. When she discovered that she could hear and understand other people, she would chat away quite happily. The 'clinging', nervous little girl was becoming a strong personality.

At the age of four years and seven months Kate joined her brothers Simon and Richard at the local convent preparatory school. The headmistress was a warm and friendly woman with a genuine love of children. Her staff, most of whom had taught there for many years, had the same qualities. The school had a marvellous happy atmosphere and parents were always made to feel welcome, so it was with ease that Kate made the transition to school life. She would feel very grown-up accompanying her brothers, aged five and six, to school. Every afternoon I would take them with Anna to the local park where they spent an hour in the children's playground, which they loved; then it was back for children's television, supper and bed. What happy carefree days they were!

Kate grew into a confident, happy little girl, with common sense far beyond her years. She loved to help me around the house, with the shopping and caring for her little sister. Anna, taught by Kate, knew the sounds of the letters and could read simple words before she went to school. They would spend hours playing happily together. On the occasions when I accompanied John on business trips, my mother would always hold the fort. The children adored her and she them. Granny never had problems about where to find things – Kate was always at hand to help and advise. She never needed as much sleep as the others and would often creep into her grandmother's bed at night and divulge family 'secrets' and other interesting items of news. As a result my mother was always well up-to-date with family matters!

Kate was very loving and demonstrative, not just towards me but towards her close family as well. Her relationship with her father was different. She loved him, but even as a small child she would refuse to let him do things for her. For instance, sometimes in the morning he would ask, 'Kate, can I put you to bed tonight?' and she would agree, but when bedtime came round she would say, 'I've changed my mind.' On such occasions, he would be upset and he would let her see it.

John was a disciplinarian; he expected his children to be models of good behaviour, especially at mealtimes, and to speak only when spoken to, though when they had permission to speak he would always listen attentively. He never actually pressurized them to work hard, but made it clear he expected them to give of their best. When they did well he rewarded them. By nature he was ambitious and hard working. He felt that to be rich would bring him security and freedom; with him, as with many men, his work came first and we were second in his priorities. To outsiders we were the 'ideal' family. We were young, we had four lovely children, a comfortable home, and John was successful. Our marriage appeared happy and stable. John certainly would have agreed with this. On the surface I wanted to believe it too, but underneath I resented his authoritarianism, his possessiveness of me – I was never able to do anything or go anywhere without first asking his permission, but despite this I grew from being a very shy, rather introverted person in the early days of our marriage, to being more self-confident and outgoing. I resented his over-strictness with the children, though I never remonstrated with him in front of them. I remember him saying more than once, 'I am the head of this family and therefore I am the one to make decisions.' Despite this, he could be a very loving husband and father, but I felt more relaxed during his visits abroad, and I believe the children did too.

Christmas and the weeks leading up to it was a time of great activity and excitement for the children. I too enjoyed it immensely, though I usually felt like collapsing with exhaustion afterwards. Eileen, her husband and daughters would join us for the day. My mother, more often than not, stayed with us for the festive season. Once the children had broken up for the school holidays, we always paid a visit to Harrod's toy department and nearer Christmas we would make another trip to London to see the lights and the giant tree in Trafalgar Square. Christmas Day itself usually dawned for us at 5 a.m. with the children bounding into our bedroom to show us what Father Christmas had brought them. Later in the morning we would all attend Mass, and the children would visit the crib which had been set up in the forecourt of the church. Kate, from when she was a tiny child, had a deep and abiding faith in God despite all the modern trappings surrounding this feast, and she never once forgot the true reason for celebrating it; the Christmas cards which she made herself always reflected this. The children would spend the afternoon in total secrecy, writing and rehearsing a nativity play to be performed after dinner for us adults. Once were entertained to a rock musical, written by Richard; another year they decided to give the nativity story a new slant – Jesus was born not in a stable in Bethlehem two thousand years ago, but in the back yard of the local 'Hare and Hounds'. For me the best part of Christmas was to watch the children performing not just for their own enjoyment but for ours.

For Kate Christmas had to be a perfect time – if someone didn't appear to be enjoying himself to the full she would come and tell me. She even avoided arguing with her brothers – nothing must spoil that special day.

In every way Kate was a high achiever and competitive. Her standards were very high. Before entering drama or poetry festivals she would enlist my help in improving her performance. She would work unceasingly and usually excelled on the actual day. She had a great feeling for poetry and found much pleasure in it. Towards the end of her illness poetry was to become one of the few delights in her life.

As Kate grew older there was a lot of rivalry between her and her eldest brother Simon. By now Simon and Richard had left the convent and were attending a boys' prep school. I remember an occasion when Simon, being unwell, was at home for the day with nothing much to do, and he taught himself to play Kate's recorder. Kate's fury knew no bounds when she returned home to hear her recorder being played by brother Simon!

Ice-skating was something they all loved, whether they were good at it or not. The first time I took Kate and Anna was with a couple of young friends when Kate was eight years old. I didn't skate myself, so I decided to keep my feet firmly on the ground and remain a spectator. In ten minutes from stepping on to the ice Kate was skating freely in the centre of the rink. When Simon heard this he asked me to take him skating, and announced that he was determined to learn in less than ten minutes. He did! – in eight minutes actually, but without the natural ability which Kate had shown. Later she went on to excel at roller-skating, gymnastics, tennis and swimming.

In the autumn of 1973 we bought a new house only a few miles from where we lived, but further into the country. John had always hankered after a place with land. The children loved it. The house was nothing special – it was its situation that attracted us. It was also very near the new school where Catherine would be commencing the following year.

At this point Kate decided that she wished to be known by her baptismal name, Catherine, and with amazing will-power and determination she refused to respond to anyone who still called her Kate. Within a few weeks she had us all trained and from then on she was known to everyone as Catherine. I remember Simon at this time reacting by saying that he would insist on being called 'Simeus Maximus Superbus'!

Our euphoria over the new house was short-lived. Oil prices soared due to the Arab/Israeli war, there was a miners' strike, a three-day working week, and a general election, and one of the results of all this was that property prices slumped. We found ourselves with two houses, neither of which we could sell, four children at private schools and massive interest rates to pay. I was for sending the children to the local state schools but John felt this would be a sign of failure on his part. He had chosen those schools for his children and he was determined to keep them there, but our income was insufficient to pay school fees and bank interest in addition to our living expenses and we were forced to borrow money. After a nightmare of a year, we managed to sell the first house, in which we were living, and moved to the new house. Catherine was now thirteen and attending her new school. We had had to sell at a reduced price so we still owed a large sum to the bank, but we were managing to keep our heads above water. In 1976 the world seemed to crash about our ears. John, who was working for a European company, was told that he had to close the London operations. The world recession had started; we were devastated. We sold our home for a second time and in December 1976 we moved to London.

During the previous two years the strain had begun to tell on John; he was now having to make people redundant and listen to their problems, none of them ever suspecting the enormous anxieties he had himself. He had always been domineering and volatile, but now he had become more aggressive and though he never harmed us physically his behaviour was sometimes frightening. Simon and Richard were at boarding-school and escaped the worst of this; in any case, John usually managed to have more control over himself when they were around. Anna, being the youngest, was tucked up in bed and asleep when he came home from the office. It was Catherine who saw it all and suffered most.

In the summer term of 1976 Catherine begged her father to allow her to become a boarder. She was very happy at school and I believe she felt she was missing out a lot being a day girl. Despite our financial position he agreed, and Catherine became a boarder for the second half of that term. Usually she hated being away from home, even for one night, but she adapted immediately and the remaining weeks of the term were really happy for her. Academically too, she improved greatly; whereas before she had had to strive hard to do moderately well, she now seemed to be learning with greater understanding and ease. She came home for the summer holidays really looking forward to the following year, when Anna would be joining her as a boarder too. We had decided, despite the added financial strain, to let both girls be permanent boarders. We felt that with another move on the horizon it would give them more stability and security. Catherine hated the idea of moving again and resented the people who came to view our property. The thought of having to part with our beloved animals also loomed large in her mind, as it did for all of us. (We had a golden retriever called Caesar and a tabby cat called Jasper. Fortunately, we sold the house to a delightful family who asked if we would give them Caesar and Jasper. We readily agreed as it meant they could continue their free and happy outdoor lives. We arranged to 'borrow' Caesar for the occasional weekend in London.)

About two or three weeks before Catherine returned to school, this time with Anna, she developed severe digestive problems. The main symptoms were flatulence and a hard, slightly swollen abdomen, just as when she was a tiny baby. Immediately, we cut out all milk and milk products from her diet but this didn't help at all. The doctor gave her various medicines to try, without success. After about six weeks he suggested that Catherine should have a barium-meal test to check whether she had any organic disease. The barium meal took just one and a half hours to go right through her system, including the bowels; it should have taken at least twelve or thirteen hours. I then took Catherine to a well-known paediatrician, who told me that Catherine was in a very anxious state and he thought that once we had moved and settled again she would be all right. He suggested a diet with plenty of roughage to try and slow things down in her digestive system. Anna was happy in her new school but Catherine, though still doing well academically, appeared pale and tired and emotionally withdrawn.

Early in December 1976 we moved to a small flat in London.

THREE

We all felt we had been given a fresh start. The flat was small and space limited, but we felt that living in London would make up for that, as there was so much to see and do. We had paid back our debt to the bank in full and had a little left over. We all breathed a great sigh of relief – we had got over the worst, so we thought.

Christmas that year was spent for the first time at the home of my sister Eileen and her family. We followed what was now family tradition, a candlelit dinner in the evening and afterwards the children's performance of their nativity play. It was a wonderful day, made more so by John's, albeit fleetingly, relaxed and happy mood. We hadn't seen him like this for at least three years. Catherine would keep coming to me and saying, 'Isn't this wonderful, Mummy – Daddy is better.' I believed so too, and hoped and prayed that Catherine would now be over all her anxieties.

After Christmas we went on a week's skiing holiday in Italy; it was on the whole a happy time. Simon, Richard, Catherine and Anna learnt to ski quickly and thoroughly enjoyed the new experience. Catherine, however, would appear remote from us much of the time, particularly after meals when John had been infuriated by her fussiness over the food. On returning home, he took us out a couple of times for dinner, but the occasion was always spoilt by his impatience with Catherine – she would eat hardly anything at these times. John was depressed and irritable, and appeared to be getting worse. This was another great worry to me, and so it was with relief that I saw the children back to school.

It was usual for Catherine and Anna to come home for the weekends. The first three weekends of that term, I met them at Victoria Station and we took a bus home. John was often deeply depressed and full of despair. He was fighting for all that was important to him, but *against* the very people whom he held most dear. He felt nothing was safe or completely to be trusted. When his mood lifted, however, he would be really kind to us, and as it was usually long past lunch or dinner time he would insist on taking us out to eat. This was an added trauma for Catherine.

At these times I think Catherine and Anna wanted me to leave their father, but I couldn't. I believed that in time all would be well. He always insisted that I was the only one who could help him. During this time a very dear friend, Catherine's godmother, with whom I had grown up, visited us. She was deeply shocked by the whole situation, not just by Catherine's illness but by what our marriage had become. She attempted to persuade John and me that for Catherine's sake a trial separation might be the answer. We disagreed. I understood John, I knew that he felt a complete failure; his ambitions had been thwarted and he had not got a secure job. He felt the world was against him and that it was our duty to comfort him and to suffer with him. To try to reason with him was futile. Invariably it sparked off another outburst and I would try and avoid this at all costs. He frightened me but, for the sake of the children, I would try and make our home life as normal as possible. I would say to them, 'Daddy will be better when he is settled in a permanent job.' At work he had the highest standards and was a good manager of people, but he failed to see what was happening to Catherine.

It was at this time that the headmistress telephoned me to tell me of her concern over Catherine's lack of eating. To my horror, Catherine told me, on arriving home, that she had not eaten or drunk for a whole week – since the previous traumatic weekend, in fact. I talked to her, cuddled her, tried to persuade her to accept some food. She told me she was frightened to swallow, indeed she insisted she could not swallow. I rang the paediatrician. He told me it was an emergency; I was to see that Catherine rested and keep trying to get her to accept some liquid. Meanwhile, he would arrange for Catherine to be seen by a specialist.

On the morning of 11 February 1977, I took Catherine to see a psychiatrist, a professor at a London teaching hospital. John said that he would come too, but although he insisted, I wanted to be sure that Catherine saw the psychiatrist alone, so that she could be more outspoken about her fears and her feelings. He would then have a clearer picture of all the circumstances and be in a better position to give help.

Catherine herself was adamant that she did not want her father to come. We left the flat quickly and caught a taxi to the hospital. On arrival, I explained to the receptionist that it was essential for my daughter to see the professor alone and asked her to get my husband to wait at the desk if he inquired for us. The waiting-room was further along the corridor and so it was possible for us to be there without John knowing where we were. Deep down I believe John felt threatened in some way and didn't want Catherine to be able to talk freely about how she saw our family problems. The professor saw Catherine for about an hour by herself. She said to me afterwards that she had told him everything. He talked to me on my own as well and I was able to give him an outline of Catherine's childhood, her eating problems and the situation at home for the previous three years. I also said that John was probably sitting at the reception desk at that moment, and he rang the receptionist and asked John to join us. He then chatted to us together and in his summing up he said that Catherine's inability to eat was a form of protest, and because eating had never been a pleasure for her, it was the easiest form of protest for her to adopt. He added that if in the next few days she had still not eaten, he would have to admit her into hospital. We agreed that I would phone him the following Tuesday.

On the journey home we decided I should take Catherine away for two or three days. On reflection I felt that I had tried to 'cover up', to make things appear as normal as possible at home, and in fact I hadn't succeeded at all – if I had been successful then Catherine would not be suffering. Catherine was happy at the idea of the two of us being together and suggested we should find somewhere to stay not too far from London but in the country. Next morning we set off and by lunch time we had settled into a delightful old-world hotel. That afternoon was bitterly cold so we sat by the roaring log fire and talked and talked. The one subject we didn't discuss was food – I had decided to avoid it for the time being. I did, however, order tea and sandwiches for myself in the hope that Catherine would share them with me. She didn't. Later that evening we went into the restaurant for dinner, but she still refused to eat. I didn't press her. That night Catherine slept with me, as the only room we could have had a double bed. I was awakened in the early hours of the morning by her sobbing. I took her in my arms and cradled her like a baby; after some time her sobs subsided and we started to talk again. This time she expressed all her fears: her apprehension whenever her father voiced his anger or frustration, her unhappiness because he couldn't understand her depression and inability to eat, and her anxiety over whether he would find another job. I told her that I felt the same fears as she did, but that we would cope with the situation together from then on; I would no longer try to help him on my own. I assured her that despite everything he loved her and me and Simon, Richard and Anna dearly. I suggested that if she was to be able to cope then she had to be well and suggested she should gear herself to eating again, say by breakfast on Monday morning. She didn't answer either way and soon we both fell asleep.

The next day she told me she had decided to try and eat something for breakfast on Monday morning, but that night she couldn't sleep for thinking about it and she experienced feelings of panic. I calmed her down and eventually she slept. Monday morning came. I ordered my usual coffee and toast and held my breath as I heard the waiter asking Catherine what she would like. To my amazement and utter relief she ordered toast, honey and hot chocolate. I made no comment – inwardly I was elated, outwardly I was calm. I asked her what she would like to do that day. I was prepared to stay away with her for several days if necessary, until I felt she had re-established her eating, but she told me she would like to return home.

On the return journey we lunched in Windsor; she was relaxed and seemed to be enjoying herself. She was still physically weak so a walk round the town was out of the question. As we got nearer home she became much quieter and then she told me that she didn't want her father to see her eating. I agreed to explain this to him. When I did he was adamant that Catherine had to eat with us; personally, I didn't care if Catherine ate every meal alone, just so long as she ate. Since John felt so strongly about this, I sent Catherine to stay with my mother on the east coast of Kent – Catherine adored her grandmother and had spent many happy holidays there – but within three days my mother telephoned to say that Catherine had stopped eating again. As I had rung the professor at the hospital in the meantime and told him I thought Catherine was going to be all right, I now had to contact him again to say that Catherine was back to square one.

Catherine was admitted to hospital towards the end of February. Although she had been depressed and withdrawn, all had gone well until the nurse who was admitting her explained, 'At mealtimes you will start off on single portions, then these will be increased to double portions.' Catherine, who had been sitting quietly on the bed, started to plead with me to take her home. Gradually her pleas turned to screams. She was panic-stricken, her cries grew louder and she became hysterical. She clung to me with such strength that it took several nurses to drag her away from me. As long as I live that scene will never leave me. Up to that day I had never heard of anorexia. Several days later Catherine asked one of the nurses what this word that everyone was using meant. He was incredulous: 'You mean you don't know what the matter is with you?'

Catherine's normal weight was established as eight stone, and this was to be her 'target' weight while she was in hospital. It was to be achieved by a punishment/privilege regime; whenever a patient gains weight he or she is allowed a privilege and as the weight goes up, the patient has more privileges – being allowed to go to the bathroom instead of having to use a bedpan, walking around the ward, wearing one's own clothes, having visitors. On the other hand, when weight is lost, privileges are denied.

Catherine reached her target weight and was allowed to join us for a holiday in Spain that Easter. During her stay in hospital no psychotherapy had been given. That spring and summer her weight stabilized at about seven and a half stone. Physically, she was well, but mentally she suffered from lack of confidence, depression and loneliness. In the past, she had always been popular at school and had always had close friends; indeed she had been joint head girl of her preparatory school and joint head girl of the junior house of her senior school. But now she was becoming more and more withdrawn. The more she felt her friends did not understand her, the more unhappy, lonely and isolated she became. For the next seven years Catherine was never to be really happy and carefree again.

When Catherine was discharged from hospital that first time – and indeed on subsequent occasions – Simon, Richard and Anna would assume that she was better because her weight was back to normal, and there would be sighs of relief all round. Increasingly though, they found her withdrawn and uncommunicative. One day Anna, on entering the bedroom which she shared with Catherine, saw 'I am ugly' written in lipstick on the mirror. Anna was desperately missing the sister whom she used to have fun with; she was embarrassed by Catherine's frequent absences from school and began to feel that her sister was 'different'.

In September 1977 Catherine became a day girl at her school, seeing the professor at the hospital about once every two weeks. Her depression was acute. With other people she was moody and difficult. It was as though all she had experienced had made some sort of assault on her mind. She had to condition herself to do anything, especially to eat. Someone close to me suggested that I force her to eat normally. I decided, against my better judgement, to give it a try. I would place a plate of food, consisting of meat or fish and vegetables or a pasta dish, in front of Catherine, and I would insist that she ate it. The ensuing scenes were more than I could bear and as a result I felt for a short time that she had lost her trust in me.

It was at about this time that she expressed a wish to learn to speak French fluently and became interested in the idea of going to school in France. Both Catherine and I felt that a complete break from home might be beneficial. Through the convent she was attending it was arranged for her to transfer to their mother house in Amiens. The professor did not entirely approve but I felt that a complete change and a challenge of Catherine's own choosing could only do good. John and I took her to Amiens in January 1978. She settled into her new environment extremely well. She appeared to have a renewed interest in everything and her progress in French was excellent.

In March she returned home for half term. I met her at Victoria Station and she looked healthy and happy. Her face had come alive again. She looked beautiful as she walked along the platform towards me. Thank God, I thought, she is over it. John by now had accepted a very good job abroad, and was due to take up his new post immediately after Catherine's half-term holiday. All appeared to be well, but it became obvious that Catherine wanted me to herself and that her new-found happiness was merely on the surface. I began to feel that she was putting it on for my benefit, that the depression was just waiting to rear its ugly head. She returned to France tearful and homesick. I received several frantic phone calls from her. She became depressed and ill, and I arranged for her to return home before the end of term.

Catherine's Diary

10 March 1978   *Amiens, France*

(I want to be 6st 7lb
this is a large problem)

I feel fed up and depressed with life sometimes. I feel like c.s.* It is my faith in God that stops me doing it for He gave me life and it would be the devil that would make me take it away. I don't want that because I don't follow the devil but God.

I can't explain to anyone exactly how I feel because they wouldn't understand. I feel a burden to everyone and I have been for a year. I wish to God I didn't feel like this. I'd give anything in the world to be a natural, sane girl, but it doesn't seem meant for me yet. I can't stay here at Amiens as much as I love it, because I am too depressed again and I feel insecure. I am obsessed with my weight, I can't explain fully to Mummy why I want to leave. I can only say my reasons are I'm homesick and disturbed.

I want to take my Os in November, and please God I'll succeed at them, if nothing else in life. I just want to hide from people and life and uncertainty. How can I overcome it? It is an impossible task all alone.

Mercredi, 29 mars 1978

I have done so much damage to myself with 3 overdoses (laxatives) in 3 weeks. I am, thank God, 6st 8 at the moment and intend staying like that. I dread to think what comments will be made by people when I don't return to France after Easter but I have decided it's my life and I know what I need. No matter what they say, I shan't let them worry me (I hope). I shall work for my Os and afterwards?

She subsequently explained to me that she could no

---

* Committing suicide.

longer cope with being away from home. I was her strength, she said. That spring we went away together for a week. She appeared relaxed and enjoyed her meals. Again I had hope that all would be well.

Back in London I arranged for her to attend a day-school. O levels were imminent and the professor was encouraging her to sit them. Initially she was to take eight subjects but she had missed so much school that finally she decided that she would take only French, Spanish, English and English Literature. Before many weeks had passed, however, she was back in hospital and being subjected to the same regime as before. (In November 1978, she sat her examinations in hospital and achieved A grades in French and Spanish and B grades in English.)

Looking back I believe Catherine's greatest deprivation was the denial of visitors. The effect of this was to cause her to withdraw further into herself. The hospital world became her 'territory', if you like, the place where she had no responsibility and where someone else was in charge of her eating. When finally she was allowed visitors she only wanted me; seeing others was an enormous strain on her. She couldn't bear them to see the change in her. As a result of the adherence to three large meals a day plus mid-morning and mid-afternoon snacks, she would feel bloated and ugly – her main concern was to get out and starve herself. I believe now that this treatment, which is still given more often than not, should be much slower. Instead of making the patient's normal weight the 'target', a much lower weight should be aimed at initially, and at the same time intensive psychotherapy should be given. Only when that weight has been absolutely accepted by the patient should another 'target' be set, again only a small increase, and so on, until finally the patient is ready to accept their normal weight. I cannot stress sufficiently the need for intensive psychotherapy throughout this programme from someone the patient trusts and with whom he or she has a good rapport. I also believe that visitors should be encouraged from the outset; this would help the patient to be less isolated and keep them in touch with life outside the hospital. And most important, seeing family and friends regularly while weight is being gained *very gradually* would lessen the trauma the anorectic feels.

At that time little was known about anorexia nervosa, and few people had heard of it. I felt I was floundering. If only I had known then what I know now, I might have been able to help Catherine more constructively and been able to prevent the irreversible chronic state of anorexia which later developed in her. Seeing my child so obviously suffering and being unable to help haunted me and still does. Witnessing the effect on one's family makes it a double tragedy. Simon, Richard and Anna were deeply concerned for her. Before their eyes their happy, vibrant sister had become withdrawn, morose, depressed and isolated. They couldn't communicate with her, they couldn't understand. But how could they? No one understands the enigma of anorexia nervosa.

The very name of the illness is misleading because it means a nervous lack of appetite. Nothing is further from the truth. Catherine had an unbelievable obsession with food; her body craved it constantly but her mind rejected it. She would be torn in two, one part of her urging her to eat and get well, the other part pleading with her not to eat, making her feel guilty and unclean whenever she did. She became excessively interested in food and totally preoccupied with cooking. She would prepare enormous meals for the family and insist that they ate everything, never sitting with us herself. Her tastes in food were bizarre and should anyone walk into a room while she was eating

34

she would either panic and scream or she would become secretive and pretend she hadn't been eating. I now see that there was a frenzy about her whenever she came into contact with food, whether shopping for it, cooking or eating. After her stay in hospital during the summer of 1978 she became totally addicted to laxatives and binging. Binging is a compulsion to eat, vomit, eat, vomit, which in Catherine's case would last for two, three or more hours on end. She became deceitful and cunning in trying to hide these manifestations of her illness. She became full of self-hatred.

Her weight loss at this time was excessive, and she was unable to attend school but she continued working alone for her O levels. The professor tried unsuccessfully to persuade her to return to hospital of her own free will. She refused adamantly. He felt she stood little chance of succeeding with her examinations unless she was in hospital so he sectioned her under Section 26 of the Mental Health Act. He advised me to say nothing to Catherine. I wouldn't have anyway; knowing her dread of hospital, I feared she would run away rather than face going in against her will.

The morning of 9 November 1978 dawned, the day Catherine was to be sectioned. My sister Eileen came to be with me and give me moral support. I needed it – it was to be another of those ordeals which were to feature so much in the course of her illness, but it must have been an even greater ordeal for Catherine herself. When the two doctors and a social worker arrived, Catherine knew instinctively why they were there. She was desperate. She clung to me, begging me to send them away. One of the doctors started to talk quietly, appealing to Catherine's logic and reasoning. When she had finished, Catherine, who now appeared outwardly calm, gave her reasons for *not* going into hospital. I cannot remember a word she said, for I was too upset, but she was extremely articulate and lucid in her own defence. Had she been in a court of law she would have won her case. It took the two doctors and the social worker at least two hours to persuade her to leave. Only when she knew they weren't going to let her win did she agree to go. The social worker, my sister and I drove her to the hospital. Once there all her fear and dread came to the fore; again I had to leave with her screams ringing in my ears. Late that evening, when I was sitting in the flat alone, too drained and exhausted to do anything, the doorbell rang; Catherine had returned home.

Within minutes of Catherine's arrival the hospital phoned to tell me that she had gone missing. I informed them that she was with me and promised to bring her back later that night. I explained to Catherine that responsibility for her had been taken from me and if I didn't take her back, then the hospital could ask the police to do so. She was tearful but calm. She asked me to make her some boiled rice pudding and this I did. While she ate the pudding we talked. Afterwards she allowed me very peaceably and quietly to take her back to the hospital, but insisted that I tell the nurses she had already eaten.

FOUR

It was at this time that we bought another house. John had been working in the Middle East for a year and we were gradually building up our resources again. I had been unable to find anything suitable in the area where we had lived before and where most of our friends still lived, but eventually I found one seventy-five miles from London with all the features which John had insisted upon. Catherine, Anna and I loved it. I worked really hard to ensure that all the necessary improvements were completed before he came home on leave in December, when we planned to move in. But when John saw the house he took an instant dislike to it, and what should have been a happy time wasn't. Catherine was home for Christmas, and the whole family joined us to celebrate, but the atmosphere was heavy with tension. The fact that so many of John's problems had been solved had not helped. I felt helpless – I could no longer cope with John and I was drained by Catherine's anorexia. Everything was proving too much for me.

In January 1979 John returned to Saudi Arabia. Simon returned to medical school, Richard to France where he was studying French, and Anna to her school, so Catherine and I were left together. She decided to attend a local secretarial school. She was out all day and on returning home each evening she worked industriously at her shorthand. At the weekends, if the others were not home from school, we always tried to do something interesting, like visiting old towns, historic churches or simply walking in the countryside. At times I would be furious with her because of her lack of eating, and then she would be angry with me for not understanding. Despite this her dependence on me was growing. By March she was back in hospital again, for her binging and addiction to laxatives had taken a heavy toll on her young body. John wanted Anna and I to visit him in Saudi Arabia for four weeks over the Easter period and we decided to go, as Catherine was in hospital. I arranged for Catherine to receive psychotherapy during this period of hospitalization. She still wanted to break free of the anorexia and on my last visit to her before I went abroad she said, 'This time I'll do it for you.'

In Saudi Arabia I became more and more anxious about Anna; she had lost weight and was eating food high in protein, but very little else. I kept my anxieties to myself, but I now had another reason to worry.

Although I had not been at ease while away, the time had been less stressful than I had anticipated and John had been trying hard to give us a good holiday. I was pleased to be able to give all my time and attention to Anna. We wrote every day to Catherine.

On returning to England we went straight to the hospital. I was aghast to learn that Catherine had received no psychotherapy. The professor was in America, and although he had given instructions for Catherine to receive this treatment, for some reason his instructions were not carried out. I was very upset and made it clear how very angry I felt. The result was that Catherine was then asked if she would like psychotherapy, and of course she refused point blank. Her only objective was to be discharged from hospital and be allowed to go home. Her weight was back to normal, but again she felt ugly and bloated. At these times her mental torment was at its worst.

In the June of that year she decided, after a lot of thought and discussion with me, to go to London, find herself a job and stay with Simon at the flat which he shared with two student friends. Richard was returning from his year in France and intended doing the same. I felt that to be with young people would help Catherine a great deal. She found herself pleasant work as a receptionist at a Harley Street dental surgery. She settled in well and appeared to enjoy her job. She would come home every weekend. It was at this time that I wrote to the professor at the hospital asking him to recommend a doctor in or near Harley Street who would give Catherine psychotherapy.

Catherine immediately developed a rapport with this new doctor. After each session she would ring me and insist that I make her eat when she came home. She would say 'However nasty and rude I am, whatever my reaction, you must make me eat.' At last I began to feel hopeful that after all this time Catherine would get well. One weekend she came home and told me that her doctor wanted her to write down every unhappy experience she could remember, going right back into her childhood. This was a traumatic exercise for her; it took her most of the weekend and almost all of the time she was in tears. Every instance was either connected with food or her father or both.

A big problem for her at this time was getting out of the fortnightly dinners the other girls at the surgery liked to organize. She would spend days in dread of being asked, and of course she always was. She would feel guilty if she refused the invitation, as she believed the others would consider her unfriendly and aloof. Her doctor really helped her with this particular problem and even though she dreaded these dinners she would usually go, and sometimes she could actually feel achievement at having overcome some of her fear. Simon and Richard were marvellous to her and included her in everything they did. She didn't always join in their outings, but the fact that they wanted her was very important to Catherine. Sometimes she would accompany her brothers to a pub where they would meet up with a group of young friends. But despite great kindness on the part of these young people she would feel totally isolated, unable to participate in their conversation and laughter. On these occasions, Richard would usually walk her back to the flat or, if they were some distance from home, she would take a taxi alone. She told me that at these times she never felt she belonged, she always felt 'different', an 'oddity'. Although she wanted to be left alone, at the same time she needed her friends and she desperately wanted them to understand. She realized fully how difficult she must appear, yet she would be deeply hurt if people couldn't be bothered to try and understand.

The summer before moving to London Catherine and Richard had become especially close, swimming and playing lots of tennis; he had also escorted her to her first 'grown-up' party when she was just fifteen, and told me how proud he had felt when everyone had said she was the most beautiful girl there. But he now missed the close relationship that they had had at that time.

John wanted us all to join him for the month of August in Saudi Arabia. Catherine didn't want to go and it was decided she would stay on in the flat and continue the psychotherapy sessions; at no time would she be alone, as Simon's medical-student friends, all of whom knew Catherine, would be constantly coming and going. We would be away for four weeks. Before going, I took Anna to see Catherine's doctor for her weight loss had now become noticeable. She knew that I knew she had an eating problem, but she never spoke about it. Even though I was almost out of my mind with worry, I decided that no fuss must be made. Anna was shocked and horrified at the idea of seeing a psychiatrist but whatever he said to her had a tremendous effect. From that day she increased her intake of food and included about three pints of milk a day as well. Even though she put on weight and appeared to be completely over her eating difficulties, I knew that they remained there, lurking under the surface, and so did she. It is only recently she has been able to talk freely about her 'mild anorexia'. It lasted about two years, but it was another two years at least before she would admit to having gone through it. It was an extremely difficult time for her and for me. Catherine was aware of Anna's problem from the beginning; here is a letter she wrote to Anna at that time which Anna showed me recently.

Wednesday, 30 July 1979

My darling Anne,

Evidently you are back at school now, it's not too bad! It was lovely seeing you last weekend, although I look forward to the day you are back to your old self. I don't intend that to sound mean, I understand you are going through a difficult time, we have all been through it, so you're not the only one who is suffering. I mean that to be a comfort.

You have everything going for you, the love of your family, a beautiful home, lovely school and a good education. You are head girl and vice camp leader (all your own doing) so do not wreck your life. I know what it is like, I've wasted three years of mine going in and out of psychiatric hospitals and regularly visiting psychiatrists. Please avoid this. I have to cover up what I have done in order to avoid mentioning it. Please God I am now nearly over it and beginning to live my life again. Unfortunately, all too late, I have realized that I have ruined three years of the family's life too, especially Mummy's because she has to bear the responsibility of everyone. She cannot take much more. You are worrying her too much at present and me also, she will crack up any day now. Please write and apologize

41

for your behaviour at half term, I realize that it wasn't deliberate by any means, but just explain to her in full how you feel and it will relieve her mind. That is what I do. You used to get on so well with her, but you can't even talk to one another now and it hurts her very deeply, you too maybe.

I assure you that this phase of misery will pass, you must fight it and pray to God. He will help you. Just think how marvellous you will soon feel when you can push all this to the back of your mind, you will feel a new person.

We all love you very, very much Anna darling and we will help you in any way we can, but as I have realized, you must spur yourself on.

> All my love and prayers,
> I do love you despite our ups and downs
> Catherine.

We returned home at the end of August to find Catherine looking very thin and ill. Apparently, the doctor with whom she had been having the psychotherapy had gone away on holiday with his family, and he had left Catherine in the care of a colleague. Catherine felt no rapport with the other doctor and so discharged herself from further treatment. By the time her own doctor returned she had lost so much weight that she refused to see him as she feared he would put her back in hospital. He wrote to her and phoned her, but still she wouldn't see him. Her eighteenth birthday was only weeks away and she knew she would be free of all doctors after that. She couldn't wait. Her diet at this time consisted of one apple a day.

In September Catherine gave up her job at the dental surgery and commenced a secretarial course at a well-known college in London. Her teachers were unanimous in their praise, saying she was one of the best students they had had, but Catherine became ill with a lung infection before the term was over and was unable to return to complete the year. Her weight was now an incredible 4st 12lb.

The infection cleared up with the use of an antibiotic, but Catherine was still feeling very ill. One night she told me she thought she was going to die. I insisted on phoning the doctor from whom she had received psychotherapy. I explained Catherine's condition and he asked to talk to her. He spoke to her for at least an hour, then I took the phone from Catherine and he explained that he had persuaded Catherine to go into hospital, a private one this time, the following morning. He told me that he was extremely concerned for her and that she could die at any time. Catherine was in such a state about going into hospital that she slept with me that night. In the early hours she woke me and pleaded with me not to take her to the hospital. I was adamant: how could she expect me, her mother, to allow her to die? She was going into hospital and that was that. Only those who have ever tried to argue with an anorectic can understand how futile it is. In the end she promised me that if I would cook something for her she would eat it. She also promised that from then on she would eat three meals a day and if within a fortnight she broke that promise then she would go into hospital. At about three-thirty that morning I went downstairs and cooked her an omelette and insisted on her having a slice of bread and butter as well. She ate it. Later I rang the doctor and told him of our compromise. He was not too happy, but if I had forced her to go to hospital that morning she would simply have jumped out of the car when we stopped at traffic lights, or maybe even run away before we started our journey. For the next ten days or so she ate one course three times a day. She began to look better and gained about five pounds in weight.

Then she stopped eating again when John returned home

in response to a letter I had written to him suggesting we part. He said he had been devastated to receive my letter, for he had never believed for a moment that our marriage was anything but secure. We talked endlessly, he usually taking on the role of interrogator. He wanted to give me everything if only I would stay – he claimed that he had changed for the better, and that from now on I would be free to do as I pleased. But I did not trust John's new understanding of me nor did I believe that he had changed.

I left home in early 1980. John had decided to return permanently from Saudi Arabia and we simply couldn't cope, living under the same roof. I also felt a failure where Catherine was concerned and could no longer tolerate the nightmare of her anorexia. I left, not really knowing where to go. I stayed in a hotel until I could find somewhere to rent. I kept in contact with the children, who were all very concerned for me. I wanted to be free, I wanted and needed time to think. I knew I was being utterly selfish. I had never felt that John had given me any support where Catherine's illness was concerned and I wanted to hand the whole burden of it to someone else. That that someone was Catherine's father, with whom she had always had a difficult relationship, made me feel guilty, but I pushed that out of my mind.

Catherine's Diary

January 1980

This morning I got up and tidied the house, then I had a bath and washed my hair. After lunch we went into Marlborough and did the shopping.

We received a letter from Mummy, it was a kindly comforting

letter, she has asked that we don't find out where she is. I have tried very hard at lunch and supper to increase my food intake, what will my weight do tomorrow? We took Hugo to the vet this evening. He has now had all his vaccinations. 30.5[kg].

January 1980

Today my weight was 31.00 kilos so I am very tense about it. I have reduced my fluid and food intake today. It has been a funny sort of day, though not as long as I thought it would be. I tidied the house as usual this morning and had a bath. This afternoon I worked at my tapestry and finished typing Simon's notes. Daddy and I went shopping and took Hugo with us in the car. Anna came home this evening, she is very distraught about Mummy and cannot understand why she has left. However by bedtime she seemed alright. I feel very depressed this evening it is a strain for me at present for everyone leans on me and pours out their anxieties and sorrows to me. I have no one with whom I can do this. It is hard. My laxatives have not worked very efficiently today, so that worries me. What will my weight be in the morning? Please dear God may it have dropped or at least not gone up. I can feel the need for a binge building up inside me.

January 1980

My weight was 30.8 this morning which pleased me. It has been a very emotional day though – Grand-dad died last night. He fell out of bed and had a heart attack.

Oh dear Lord please help us. Mummy is still away – what good is she doing herself? Please help us to get the family reunited very very soon. Amen. May tomorrow bring a ray of hope or light into our lives.

January 1980

My weight was 30.2 kilos today. Quite a drop from yesterday, thank goodness. I felt very relieved and pleased. I didn't swallow very much today and intend keeping my eating down to a minimum now as I want to keep my weight between 30–30.5 kilos. After lunch I drove into Marlborough and back. My driving is very much better today after so much practice yesterday!

Daddy was surprisingly in a bright mood throughout the day, which I never expected at all. Mind you, I think he suffered a slight hangover this morning! We phoned Anna this afternoon, she was very tearful and is pining madly for Mummy to come home.

January 1980

My weight was 30.2 kilos, so I felt pleased today. Not an awful lot has happened in fact – I have very little to report. Mummy rang about midday and asked Daddy to collect her. He drove her to London. Apparently, she was very tearful, however she let him take her out to dinner.

I am very depressed. I went on an enormous binge, whilst I was on my own. That didn't please me because I can really manage without that now.

January 1980

... I am in a strange mood, I feel empty and lonely. I don't understand it.

February 1980

I weighed 30 kilos only this morning, that really made my day.

I have been feeling very depressed and ill, my laxatives have made me feel very sick. Daddy left for London at about 4.30 so I then prepared my massive binge which I began at six o'clock and finished at 8.30.

I cleaned the house from top to bottom. I finished typing Simon's notes this morning.

February 1980

My weight was 29.9 kilos today. It will go up again tomorrow because it is just from dehydration after my binge yesterday. I have taken my eating carefully today because I would like to try and keep my weight down tomorrow.

... I spoke to Anna on the phone, I think she was a little tearful.

February 1980

My weight was 30 kilos this morning which pleased me. I had expected to jump up more today.

I went on a massive binge which lasted all afternoon. Afterwards I drank $1\frac{1}{4}$ bottles of soda water, 1 cup of tea and had my usual pick at a Kit-Kat. I also took a suppository and a second dose of laxatives. My stomach feels so bloated even now.

February 1980

I weighed 30.3 kilos this morning, it did not bother me too much as I now realize I must permit my self to fluctuate between 30 and 31 kilos, but I could not bear to be any more than that.

Daddy was really down this morning which made life very dull, dreary, depressing and difficult for me. Anyway, thank God, by the afternoon he had bucked up. I did loads of dictation and typing for him which passed the time.

This evening we both had one hell of a go at one another and were both very irritable.

February 1980

... I had a very busy day here, I cleared the house from top to bottom. I actually managed not to binge ... until supper time, when I went on a long binge. At first it was not very successful but then I carried out a second one and managed to clear my stomach.

February 1980

I weighed 30.1 kilos today, my binge was successful.

I went to London and had my hair cut. I then went to see Mummy, we had a reasonably good talk. I still feel so down because she feels she has made the wrong decision in coming back to Daddy. She is in a low mental state. It really does hurt me deeply ... I feel numb inside.

February 1980

I weighed 30.4 kilos today It has been a traumatic day. Daddy left early for London. I just broke down and cried out loud for ages; I can't take any more.

I had an enormous binge this afternoon, basically it is an addiction whenever I am alone in this house. I feel so down.

February 1980

I weighed 30.2 kilos today ... We met Anna, Mummy and Simon for lunch. Richard had gone to a friend for the day. It was a lovely feeling to be together ...

This evening we went to Mass at Brompton Oratory and I drove there. Mummy, Daddy and Anna couldn't believe how well I drove!

February 1980

My weight was 30.1 today, I was pleased. I have actually tried to eat a lot more today, so I will have gained weight tomorrow because I always do when I eat even a mouthful more than the previous day.

February 1980

My weight was 30.3 today ... Daddy was extremely down this morning, but gradually bucked up. He was though, very tense all day. I feel so helpless when he is like this because nothing I do or say will help him.

Anna phoned, she was a little lonely I fear and still feels insecure. Unfortunately I am in a down mood today whereby I am continuously picking at food, so I dread to think what my weight will do tomorrow.

February 1980

I weighed 30.4 today ... I feel so depressed and low, what is my future? I know that I want, more than anything, to get my secretarial qualifications and begin my career, but at the moment it doesn't look like I shall be able to start again in April, due to the family situation.

I feel everyone dislikes me as a person and I certainly dislike myself. I just pray to God that we can buy the other house and sell this.

I tried harder with my eating today. My laxatives were very effective compared with other days.

February 1980

This morning I weighed 30.5 Daddy was in a really depressed state and I just don't know how I managed to cope with him.

I met Mummy this morning, I love her so much and my love for her today was so strong. I begged her to come back to us.

When I returned home Daddy and I had a row and he just went up to bed saying that he would keep out of my way until Sunday. However that didn't last very long, he came downstairs this evening whilst I was binging. Anyway he didn't notice, so I just disappeared upstairs.

We made it up when I came down.

4 March 1980

My weight was 30.2 kilos this morning so I was really pleased, although I do now realize that the time has come when I really must put on some weight, particularly as we have sold the house and that means that we will be moving in under a fortnight. The day for exchanging contracts is this Friday.

I ate a lot more today.

During the three months I was away John sold the house and bought another in the area where we had lived before our financial troubles and Catherine's illness had started. Whenever I saw Catherine at this time she was full of praise for her father, how understanding he was, how tolerant he had become. I believed they had reached a greater understanding of each other but it was two years later that Catherine told me the truth. Her father had undergone a time of deep depression and in truth it was she who many times carried him through the black period and did so much to make a new home for us all.

Catherine's Diary

5 March 1980

I now weight 30.5 kilos. I know that I must let my weight rise, but I am scared to do so. However I feel too thin the way I am. I want to be able to wear nice clothes again. I know that I will feel better and more normal in every sense if I could put on some weight. I long to feel as a girl of my age should feel.

I took Mummy the contract to sign for the house today. I hope she decides to come back to the family. I think that she will.

March 1980

I weighed 30.9 kilos. I went to see Mummy this morning and she has told me that she is coming back to us. I am just so thrilled. She would like me to go to France with her and Anna on the 31st. I will wait and see.

50

March 1980

I weighed 30.9 kilos this morning. We left home at seven and spent the whole day in Surrey seeing builders, etc.

There is just so much to do that I feel quite depressed. Will we ever move and *get* settled again? I drove round all the old haunts and they just bring back so many memories. I long to move back there again – I really do.

April 1980

I weighed 31.9 today ... I felt in complete control after my binge today as I saw myself in the mirror – a skeleton.

April 1980

This morning I weighed 31.5 kilos. Anne gave me a real talking to about my anorexia and asked me what I was going to do about it. To be honest, I don't really know.

April 1980

This morning I could not weigh myself as Anna hid the weighing scales from me. I was panicking as I am sure I have put on some weight. However I have so far taken two lots of laxatives and shall take some more this evening after supper ...

Mummy came round at lunch time and Daddy took her out. They went to Croydon.

I went to see Mr — at Nestlé's. He was very nice, I have been offered the job and accepted it. I begin on Monday.

May 1980

This morning I weighed 32.1 kilos. I am very upset about it. That is 5st 1lb; I must lose that extra pound as I don't wish to weigh more than 5 stone. I feel very sick and full.

Out of conscience I returned to the family but felt apart from them. I was very unhappy and unable to settle to anything. One morning in July, I packed a suitcase and drove away for six weeks. I travelled around most of England, staying two or three nights anywhere that took my fancy. It was a time of great loneliness and soul-searching. During the sixth week I telephoned home and spoke to Anna. I asked, 'What are you doing?' She replied, 'I'm making a quiche for supper tonight.' When I put the phone down I knew that it should be me preparing the supper, not Anna. I knew also that I had to go home for Catherine's and Anna's sakes. Next day I left for home.

In the September of this year John was working for a company in London. Simon was due to return to medical school and commence his first clinical year. Richard had a job with a firm of estate agents and was doing well and Anna went back to school to begin her O-level year.

Catherine decided to recommence her secretarial studies. The college she had attended for so short a time the previous year agreed she could do the six months' intensive course. This would include all aspects of secretarial training and was normally reserved for university graduates. At the end of six months she was the only one to be awarded a first-class diploma. During this period her weight had stabilized at five stone. She would never eat with the family and rarely had the same food as anyone else. She would cook enormous amounts of food of her own choice and then just pick at it. The cooking and picking at the food was an important ritual and no one was allowed in the kitchen at these times. It was a great strain on everyone.

The following January, three months before she qualified as a secretary, a friend gave me the name of a doctor who had had some success in the treating of anorexia. I passed the information on to Catherine who said she wasn't interested in seeing any doctor. However, shortly afterwards she made an appointment and asked me to go with her. The doctor gave her a thorough physical examination and was appalled at Catherine's condition. She agreed to accept Catherine for treatment, which was to be a form of antidepressant drug and hormone therapy. In the case of a girl who was addicted to at least seventy laxatives a day the treatment didn't stand much chance of success, because the drugs would not remain long enough in her system to bring about the desired effect. Catherine only tried it for two or three weeks, then discharged herself. I never believed the treatment would work for Catherine, though I kept these thoughts to myself since I was relieved that she was seeing a doctor once more. My relief didn't last long.

Within one week of completing her secretarial course she found herself a job as a secretary to three directors of an export firm in the heart of London. She was in charge of running the office, arranging their trips abroad, organizing hotels and appointments for customers visiting London and operating the telex machine. All in all it was a taxing and challenging job for a young newly qualified girl but she did it efficiently and enjoyed it. Her hours were from 9.30 to 5.30 five days a week. She rarely left the office before 6.30 or 7 p.m. It was a long and arduous day for someone in Catherine's low physical state, but her mental alertness and energy carried her through. Though she was pitiably thin, weighing only five stone, she still retained her facial beauty. She would dress well and cleverly to hide her thinness. Her whole life revolved around work and home; at home her life was regulated by a strict

53

routine. Apart from work and family her life was one of total isolation. She placed great dependence on me and needed all the love and patience that I could give her.

For about a year Catherine kept a record of the food she prepared for herself. I must explain that the only time she swallowed solid food was during a binge. At all other times she would chew the food, then remove it from her mouth and place it in a basin. Should she be eating anywhere outside her home, then the basin was replaced by a 'secret' plastic bag, or sometimes her pockets.

The very repetitiveness of the following pages reveals the extent of her obsession with food and weight.

Catherine's Diary

August 1980

I have never felt as ill and weak today since last November. How I survived work I will never know.

25 June 1981

Mood	: Mixed
Weight	: 31.2 kilos
Breakfast	: Tea. Kit-Kat
Lunch	: Tea, soda-water, Kit-Kat, 2 cinnamon danish, 1 cheese
Supper	: 2 rolls, cheese dish, 1 Kit-Kat, tea
Binge	: Bread, crisps, popcorn, swiss rolls, sugar puffs, remainder of supper cheese dish.
Laxatives	: 105 this morning and evening (work)
Remarks	: Not too bad a day. Gilly and Anna finished their O levels and came home. Daddy not really speaking to me. I binged because I just felt obsessional.

26 June 1981

Mood   : Abnormally cheerful
Weight   : 31.1
Breakfast : Kit-Kat and tea
Lunch   : Tea, soda water, Kit-Kat, 2 cinnamon, 1 cheese.
Supper   : Tea, Kit-Kat, 2 sausage rolls, spring greens, mashed potato (knowing I could binge later).
Binge   : Spring greens, sausage rolls, potatoes (boiled and mashed), toast, apple pickings, cottage cheese pickings, shreddies.
Laxatives : 109 approx. morning and evening (work)
Remarks   : Not too bad a day. I knew the family would be going out this evening about 9 o'clock so I had supper about 7.50 and then binged later when they were out. I felt quite cheerful today but deep down I feel a wave of depression and am waiting for it to break out. It could be a few days, one can never tell with me.

28 June 1981

Mood   : Depressed
Weight   : 30.4
Breakfast : 1½ Kit-Kats, tea.
Lunch   : Cornish pasty, 2 sausage rolls, cheese dish, tea, 1½ Kit-Kats.
Supper   : Roast beef, cabbage, boiled new potatoes, Yorkshire pudding, gooseberry fool and 1½ Kit-Kats, tea.
Binge   : I began at 4.00 and finished 7.30. Bread, sausages, cheese, sugar puffs, sweets, bonbons then a second one on Twiglets, cheese puffs, sweets and crisps.
Laxatives : 145 approx.
             51 this morning, 93/4 evening 7.30.
Remarks   : This morning I really broke down and sobbed my heart out to Mummy and Daddy. I have just given

55

up hope of ever getting better. Mummy, I am sure, is the only person who can help me. I had a dreadful afternoon binging and I have no idea how much food I retained in me, but it feels a lot. I weighed 31.00 kilos after it. It is now 11.30 and the extra laxatives are not having much effect. My stomach is bloated and full of wind. May I have not gained tomorrow. I am so scared and mentally torn inside. Dear Jesus, please help me.

29 June 1981

Mood	: Fair
Weight	: 30.9 – 31.2?
Breakfast	: Kit-Kat, tea
Lunch	: Tea, soda water, Kit-Kat, 2 cinnamon, 2 cheese danish
Supper	: Pasty, sausage roll, cheese dish, Kit-Kat, tea.
Binge	: Ryvita, 1 biscuit, cornflakes, crisps, potato.
Laxatives	: 110 approx.
Remarks	: I have a splitting headache. I am disturbed by my weight. It is not as bad as I expected, but nevertheless it is not good. This evening Daddy is away. I really feel desperate. I so wanted to talk to Mummy but we hardly said a word to each other until after my binge.

Oh! I do love her so much.

1 July 1981

Mood	: Fair, but low this evening
Weight	: 31.1
Breakfast	: 1½ Kit-Kats, tea.
Lunch	: Tea, Kit-Kat, 2 cinnamon, 1 cheese danish
Supper	: 2 sausage rolls, cheese dish, tonic water, tea, Kit-Kat

Binge   : 4 brown rolls toasted with spreads, biscuits, cereal,
           crisps: 2nd time, crisps, oranges-sucked, cheese
           dish, ham, chocolate and choc. cakes.
Laxatives : 108 approx.
Remarks : I really had intended not to binge tonight and until
           10.30 I felt OK. My laxatives worked efficiently due
           to exercise. My binge lasted from 10.30 until 2.40
           a.m. Help! Daddy was needling me tonight and
           Mummy was cross with Hugo. She did some baking
           for her coffee morning tomorrow.
               I felt tearful and depressed tonight.

4 July 1981

Mood   : High (low this evening)
Weight   : 30.4
Breakfast : $1\frac{1}{2}$ Kit Kats, tea
Lunch   : Salad, egg, tea.
           Tea-time: tea, cheesecake.
Supper   : Sausage roll, cornish pasty, cheese dish, tea, $\frac{1}{2}$ Kit-
           Kat
Binge   :
Laxatives : 110 approx.
Remarks : I went to London today and had my hair cut.
           Mummy and I had a lovely day shopping. My
           laxatives didn't work until 5.45 and I only passed
           water twice throughout the day. I do not intend to
           binge tonight so I daresay I will weigh more
           tomorrow.
               Anna came home, but went out this evening
           with Finula
               I dread my weight tomorrow.

7 July 1981

Mood   : Mixed. High/Low
Weight   : 30.2
Breakfast : 1½ Kit Kats, tea.
Lunch   : 1½ Kit-Kats, tea, soda water, 3 cinnamon.
Supper   : 1 sausage roll, 1 pasty, potatoes, cheese dish, tea.
Binge   : Supper incorporated, 2 boiled eggs, bread, Dutch
           crisp bakes, mousaka, cereal, 2nd mousaka,
           potatoes, Dutch crisp bakes, bread, sweets.
Laxatives : 110 approx.
Remarks : My binging went on the whole evening and when
           Mummy and Daddy arrived home I still had not
           finished. I don't feel that I managed to get it all up.
           Hence, what will my weight do tomorrow?

23 July 1981

Mood   : Fair
Weight   : 31.4
Breakfast : 1 Kit-Kat, tea
Lunch   : 2 cinnamon, 2 cheese, Kit-Kat, Fresca, tea.
Supper   : 3 sausage rolls, cheese dish, Kit-Kat, tea.
Binge   : Marmite and mustard on rye bread, French toasts,
           Frosties.
Laxatives : 115 approx
Remarks : Daddy was away tonight. I binged, am feeling low
           but cannot cry to ease it.

In October 1981, when she had held her job for six months, her physical condition began to deteriorate further. She experienced great pain in the lower part of her back and generally felt very ill. She refused absolutely to see a doctor. She was due for two weeks' holiday and had been planning it and looking forward to it for some time. As a twentieth-birthday present John offered to pay for her to spend a week visiting Venice and Florence. She asked me to accompany her. We planned to have three or four days in Paris, a city she loved, in the second week. I tried to persuade her to see a doctor before we left and to have blood tests done; if the results were all right we would go. She refused. Simon, understanding what happens to the human body when there is excessive weight loss, was even more concerned. Eventually she agreed to allow him to take a blood sample and have it analysed at the hospital where he was a student. He turned up at her office one lunchtime when no one else was there and acquired his sample. Catherine was quite impressed, as no one before had accomplished the procedure easily; being so under-weight her veins tended to collapse and it could take up to an hour for the blood to be obtained. Simon had managed it in a minute or two! The sample was analysed and, though her blood count was low, it was not dangerously so. The trip was on.

Venice is one of my favourite cities and it was with joy that I introduced it to Catherine. The weather was cool but ideal for sightseeing. We stayed in a small hotel just ten minutes' walk from St Mark's Square. Our room was at the top of the building and it was with difficulty that Catherine climbed the stairs to reach it. We ate all our meals in the hotel; this was less of an ordeal for her as the food was put in front of her. She played at eating it but actually was putting the food into a plastic bag hidden under the napkin on her lap. She was an expert at this, and even someone watching her very carefully would not catch her doing it.

She lapped up the beauty of Venice, the architecture, museums, shops and its special atmosphere. Our visit there was a success; her routine had not been too different from

59

what it was at home and so she had been able to cope. Our three days in Venice over, we took the train to Florence. This journey disrupted her routine and as a result she became agitated, panicky and physically weakened. The hotel in Florence provided only bed and breakfast. I thought at first that this would be better for Catherine, but in her state deciding on where to have lunch and what to have (even though she would only swallow a few crumbs) was momentous. She would insist on going inside numerous cafés and looking at the selection of cakes and pastries. By her second day she decided a pastry was what she *had* to have for lunch. If she didn't see *exactly* what she wanted, the hunt would be continued, sometimes for two hours. When we did find what she wanted she would be unable to face it, and would usually break down in tears. On the way back to the hotel she would be full of apologies and beg me to understand. We talked about her break with routine and how it affected her. One evening I suggested that she decide then and there where we would have lunch the following day, and for the rest of the time we were in Florence, and then she could gear herself up to going there. This she agreed to try. The last couple of days in Florence were easier and more enjoyable as a result, although all the time I was becoming more alarmed at her condition and fearful that she might collapse before we returned home. The trip to Paris was off; there was no way that Catherine could have undertaken it – she was very ill and was actually admitting it.

Simon had spoken to one of his professors about Catherine, and he promised to see Catherine the moment she agreed to see him. Two days after returning from Italy Catherine said she would see the professor; he examined her that same day and spent at least two hours trying to persuade her to remain in hospital. She told him she would go home and think about it, and would probably come back the next day. Both he and I knew that once she had left the hospital she would not return – we were proved right. He wrote to her explaining her urgent need of treatment, but nothing would induce her to go into hospital. She had to resign from her job as she no longer had the strength even to get on a train. It was about this time that she decided she no longer wanted to live; she constantly talked of death as being her only means of release from anorexia. She told me that she was now addicted to one hundred laxatives a day. The binging syndrome had returned, and she feared and dreaded it. She suffered blackouts and feelings of loathing and hatred towards herself. The agony and torment are indescribable.

Catherine's Diary

Monday, 4 January 1982

I woke up at 6.15 and went through my normal ritual of getting up, having my breakfast and reading the paper. I was really prepared to go into hospital today, I had got everything ready and everyone has been so fantastic in helping me prepare for it. I am so scared tonight because I did not go and have lost my nerve for going in. If only I could have smoked, but I couldn't possibly have given that up as well as my laxatives, Kit-Kats, routine and freedom. Worst of all I know deep down that I will never be able to eat or face gaining weight, but at least had I gone, I would have felt I had given it a try. I can just see how everything is going to go now. Daddy will never smile or do anything to please me. He will pressurize me and I cannot face that. If only he would understand that it really is not my choice that I should die, but that I am trapped. In the forefront of my mind is the fact that I know I can never eat and gain weight. I am just fooling myself.

I feel so selfish after all that has been done for me. I will now take a back seat and live in my room, taking my tea to my room and not cooking supper. I do not want to be a burden or an irritation to anyone anymore; besides I have caused many problems in the past and am causing more now. If I keep out of the way the better it will be for all concerned. I have decided to cut down on my intake of food, not that that is very possible as I eat so little anyway.

I just pray that I do not live for another two months but die very soon. I know I am a selfish person at present and a big coward. The sooner I go the better. I cannot face the guilt that I feel at the moment. I was prepared to go into Barts, I really was and when I have my mind made up to do something and things don't go that way, it is just too much. For the first time ever today I realized death is inevitable. I feel helpless and trapped.

Wednesday, 6 January 1982

I woke up with a start at 7.15 and rushed downstairs because I thought that my breakfast might clash with Daddy leaving for work. I received a 'thank-you' letter from Granny. I feel terrible because I just cannot write to anyone at present. I have lost my concentration. My mind feels numb and today I felt like a rag doll that had lost its stuffing. I cannot cope with the change in my regime. I know in my heart of hearts that I will die. Hospital will do no good, I cannot bear to leave home. I just pray that I am left in peace to die. I want no more pressures from anyone, it puts me in a state of turmoil so that I don't know where to turn.

Saturday, 16 January 1982

Today was one of my worst days for a long time. This morning I went into Croydon, Mummy drove me. I bought a bath robe and some magazines and then I came home. This outing unsettled me because it is not usual. This afternoon I was in mental agony. I just felt like eating and binging. Binging is the only way I have of remaining in my own world and of being able to indulge in food, thus taking my mind off everything, particularly my problems. Vomiting uses up my mental and physical energy, sometimes it leaves me hyperactive, but today it left me feeling drowsy. I am so restless and unhappy I cannot go on. I don't know what will happen. I just know that I cannot face hospital.

Wednesday, 27 January 1982

I have never felt so low and depressed as I did today. I feel so trapped. I want to live for my family's sake but I cannot live with myself. Anna was so sweet this evening, she came and sat next to me and just hugged me, this helped me. Daddy was so sweet too and Mummy as always, a tower of strength. Father Taggart came today and gave me Holy Communion.

I keep waking up at night – I have these bad dreams of intruders in the house.

Oh I do need help and love at home, and I get it, but I cannot help feeling very low.

The routine was all-important to her. She would rise early each morning, the effort to get up becoming harder each day, but forcing herself to do so. She bathed at the same time each day. Her room, which she would insist on cleaning herself, was cleaned thoroughly each day and always at the same time. If she wore something, say, a blouse, for only one or two hours, it had to be washed. Her eating, or should I say picking at food, occurred three times a day at exactly the same time. Her food fads at this time were sausage rolls, cornish pasties and Kit-Kats, and she drank black coffee. If for any reason she was five minutes late commencing her so-called 'meal' she would panic, cry and more often than not be unable to touch it.

If this happened she would try and establish a new fad, and it would sometimes take her a couple of days to do this. In the meantime, apart from black coffee, she would have nothing at all. All this went on for five months – months when I didn't know if she would live from one day to the next. During these months our GP, Dr Margaret Foot, visited regularly. She was the one doctor that Catherine consented to see. Catherine would always see Dr Foot alone, but invariably told me what they had talked about later in the day. A strong friendship developed between them and Catherine loved and trusted her. Dr Foot told me to phone her at any time should Catherine or I feel the need to talk to her, or if an emergency arose, and her support was a great source of strength to me.

Catherine's Diary

Sunday, 31 January 1982

... Anna was so sweet and said 'don't worry Catherine, you cannot help getting like this'. I told Richard how I love him even though I may not show it. I have been wanting to say that to him for a long time now.

Friday, 5 February 1982

... I cried to Anna when she came in. Simon and Jenny came and brought me the most beautiful bunch of flowers, these gestures mean more than anything to me.

Wednesday, 11 February 1982

... Oh Jesus help me. I can do nothing. I am worn out with life. Please do things for me your way.

64

With Daddy away I am able to lie in all this week. I felt quite chirpy this morning because I always look forward to being able to talk to Dr Foot, I find it such a relief. She examined my heart today, it is the same as before. It amazes me that I am still alive because by looking at me medically speaking it would seem impossible for my body to tick over. She says that it is a question of mind over body. The fact that I still have hope that I will miraculously be able to face treatment one day is evidently what is keeping me alive. She gave me a prescription for some antidepressants ...

My feelings at this time were ones of anger, compassion, love and determination that she should not die. There were moments when the suffering was so much I couldn't bear it, and I would beg God to take her. These times never lasted for more than minutes, always I felt that I had to infuse into Catherine my desire for her to live. I would say to her, 'Catherine, life is worth living, even if it is hard – we're here for such a short time. Give it a try.' Always her answer was, 'If I could, I would do it for you.' Sometimes I would break down and then she would comfort me. Simon and Richard came home every weekend. I remember my mother saying to Simon, 'You never visit me now' – 'No, Gran,' replied Simon, 'Mum needs me, I have to go home as often as possible.'

Simon was studying for his pathology examination, and I went to see him not long before he sat the exam. I had a supply of home-cooked food for him as I wanted to be sure he ate properly and sensibly at the time. We talked of Catherine. For quite a while he had believed Catherine to be bloody-minded and awkward; now he understood the seriousness of her illness. He completely broke down, the first time I had seen him break down on his sister's account.

He asked me to buy Catherine something. When I refused to take the money he said, 'You have saved me a lot bringing me all this, I want Catherine to have something from me.' I believe he was desperately trying to tell Catherine how much he loved her.

Catherine's Diary

I just don't know what to do. I want to be kept happy so that my will and hope for a miracle will be kept alive. I so need to be showered with love ...

Monday, 1 March 1982

I was feeling very depressed today. When Dr Foot came I just wanted to break down and cry. I just couldn't open up and talk. When she had gone, I so wanted her to come back so that I could unburden myself to her ... I know I won't die yet, I just know it and I really do want to so very much now. I cannot face hospital but how much longer am I going to go on living this type of existence? I can't bear it; I had a long chat with Mummy after lunch. It eased me a little. This evening I just locked myself away and binged. I weighed 26.9 afterwards and finished at approx. 12.30 a.m. I eventually got into bed at about 1.30.

Catherine was adamant about never seeing another psychiatrist, but in January 1982 Dr Foot persuaded her to meet a consultant physician. He came to the house, and Catherine liked him immediately, but she refused to have any kind of treatment. After some weeks Dr Foot and the consultant finally persuaded Catherine to go into hospital; this time she was to have a room in the medical wing of a private hospital which was run by nuns, although the majority of the staff were lay people. Despite the love, care and kindness given to Catherine she still refused treatment. Within two or three days of going in she established her routine. One of the most important times in the day for her was choosing her lunch and dinner from the menus. She would tick off what she wanted and nearly always added notes about how the food was to be cooked. She even asked to see the catering manager in order to explain to him some of her problems.

Catherine's Diary

Monday, 5 April 1982

I arrived at St Antony's Hospital with Mummy and Daddy at about 2.45 p.m. We had a very warm welcome, and it really is a lovely place. I have my own room with a shower and toilet en suite, remote-control colour TV, radio and an electronic bed. The staff are very kind and warm. I don't feel institutionalized or as though I am in hospital. For supper I had fried fillet of plaice and mixed vegetables followed by cheese and biscuits and a cup of tea with my Kit-Kat. Mummy, Richard and Anna came this evening. At 9 p.m. I had some Bovril, then at 9.30 I had 2 Kit-Kats and cup of tea. I had a bath and then just pottered around before I went to bed. The doctor came to see me at 7.30 and made me feel very relaxed. He prescribed some Valium for me and some other tablets. He is going to have me connected to a cardiac machine tomorrow also, I am to have several other tests carried out. At 3.30 p.m., $1\frac{3}{4}$ after my lunch, I weighed in at 27.2 kilos.

Each morning she would write out a timetable for her day, and this had to be rigorously adhered to. If the nurse was five seconds late bringing her medicine she would be distressed and ring the bell to remind her. Friends would have to let Catherine or me know when they intended visiting; if they were at all late she would become anxious and agitated. She found it very difficult to see people and usually saw only close family and those for whom she had a special affection. I would leave home at ten o'clock in the morning and stay with Catherine until four in the afternoon, leaving her alone only while she ate her lunch. At this time, she would allow no one, not even me, to see her eat. She was now becoming expert at chewing food, but never swallowing anything solid. Here, in hospital, she didn't feel any necessity for plastic bags because she could simply return the chewed food to her plate and, before her tray was removed, cover the plate with the lid which had been used to keep the food hot while it was brought to her. I did everything I could to try to persuade her to accept tube feeding. (This method involves a tube being passed from a bottle containing nourishment to the stomach via the nose and throat. It's not as uncomfortable as it sounds.) I believed that she would put on weight more slowly, and this would be less traumatic for her than the treatment she had previously received in hospital. Intravenous feeding (being fed by drip directly into a vein) was never considered for Catherine, as she would simply have disconnected herself; also, because of her poor physical state, the risk of infection would have been high. Her consultant, whom she trusted implicitly, played his part with great patience in trying to win her round to the idea of being tube fed. Always she said she would think about it, and at times came very close to agreeing to it but, alas, she never did.

Simon and Jenny, a fellow medical student, were due to be married in June just nine weeks after Catherine's admittance to hospital. Catherine was overjoyed at the prospect of the wedding and thoroughly approved of her sister-in-law to be. At first, Jenny had found Catherine's anorectic obsessions extremely difficult to tolerate. It seemed such a silly phenomenon and beyond understanding how anyone could dislike eating. She also felt it was incongruous that while there are young people with malignant disease who do not want to die, here was someone choosing, as it seemed to Jenny, to starve herself and partially destroy the family and those who loved her. Gradually though, she discovered the very loving and generous nature which lay behind the selfish, determined anorectic side of her character.

Catherine's Diary

Thursday, 6 May 1982

I woke up after a not too good night's sleep. Everything went according to schedule this morning. The doctor came in at 10.00 and we chatted about tube feeding. I felt very calm and placid this morning. In my own mind I know I will never eat without help and that therefore tube feeding is the only way I will survive, but it will be another week or two before I can begin. I know that I can only accept it when I feel ready. I told the doctor this. He said my heart would probably be all right while I sat here. He is concerned about the electrolyte system in my body. I really got into my knitting before lunch. Lunch was late and I felt myself getting really agitated. After lunch I was all shaky and zombie-like, my speech was slurred. Lizz came at 1.40. I felt so embarrassed, her seeing me the way I am. I felt I had really wasted her day off. Jane rang this evening, she said she would come to see me this weekend if I was making progress. She won't be pleased when I cannot give her a date on which I will start tube feeding. I reckon it will be 2–3 weeks, at least, but it is better that way, than before I am ready. It is my mental state,

I actually can feel my body packing up now. I know in myself that time is running out.

Once again I am writing my diary, it has been a few days since I last wrote it, but I have been so depressed. I will not die, but just sit here getting no better until the money runs out. I look back and see just how little progress I have made and can never go home until I am well. I have asked Mummy to telephone the doctor and explain to him exactly how I feel, before I see him tomorrow. I just don't know what to do or where to turn any more. I can't open the door to life ...

The wedding was very important to Catherine and was the thing which kept her going, though she felt she would be unable to attend herself because the idea of being with so many people terrified her. Then just one week before the wedding Catherine told me she wanted to be a bridesmaid! Both families were deeply concerned; we wanted nothing to spoil Jenny and Simon's day and Catherine, as well as being extremely weak, was by this stage incontinent. I knew that if Catherine made up her mind then she would carry out her task successfully. It says much for Jenny's understanding and generosity that she agreed. Catherine only wanted to be at the church service; she knew, as we all did, that that would be all that she would be capable of doing.

So on 5 June, a beautiful hot, sunny day, Catherine was collected from the hospital by two young friends, one a recently qualified doctor, and driven the fifty miles or so to Jenny's home where I was waiting to help her dress for the big event. She was very difficult and moody. I remember her constantly imploring me not to send her back to the hospital. When ready she joined the other bridesmaids,

Jenny's three sisters and Anna. The service went without a hitch, Catherine crying quietly throughout. She was filled with a mixture of emotions, sorrow at not being truly able to be part of the proceedings and indeed, of life itself, and joy at seeing her brother married. Once the service was over and the photographs taken, including a number of Instamatic photographs for her to show the nurses, she was taken back to hospital by the two girls who had so kindly brought her.

From the moment she returned to her hospital room she withdrew totally into herself. The dress and photographs which she had promised to show the nurses were hidden away. The occasion for which she had longed and looked forward to for many months was over. Now she was determined to die. Her condition deteriorated mentally and physically. Less than two weeks after the wedding John and I were called at 3.40 in the morning – Catherine was dying. Within twenty minutes we were there. I jumped out of the car before John had fully come to a halt and rushed through the hospital doors. I went into her room and sat beside her, placing my head on the pillow next to hers. 'Catherine,' I whispered, 'it's me, Mummy.' I willed her to live, to get well; I prayed as I had never prayed before. Slowly her arm went around my neck. She was completely unaware of everything – she remembered nothing afterwards – yet I believe in her subconscious she knew I was with her. The consultant arrived and took charge. John and I waited in the next room while he examined Catherine and finally managed to insert the tube into her nostril and down her throat. She was being tube fed. I cannot remember how much time passed until she regained consciousness but when she did she was panic-stricken that the dreaded tube was down. With very slow but deliberate movements she tore at the plaster that was holding the tube to her nose and pulled the tube out. I rushed from the room and called the consultant, but nothing he or I could say or do would persuade her to be fed in this way. I remained in the hospital with Catherine for nine days and nights; no one believed she would pull through, but she did. She now weighed about three and a half stone.

FIVE

Gradually, Catherine's mental energy returned but she was even more moody, more depressed, more demanding and difficult, and more full of resentment than ever before. When she was at her worst she would explain that there was an 'evil' presence around her. She would be terrified and ask me to pray with her. The prayers would gradually restore an element of peace within Catherine, but she would always be in dread of another attack from this 'evil'.

Initially when Catherine had become addicted to compulsive binging and vomiting it had acted as a release for much of her pent-up anxiety, but now it was something she feared more than anything. While the binging urge was at its height, she would go to enormous lengths to obtain food. For instance, she phoned a local taxi service, gave a large shopping list for food (and laxatives) and asked for it to be brought round to her room at the hospital. This worked a couple of times, until the sister-in-charge discovered what was happening. The worst time of the day was after supper when the craving would frequently come upon her. Sometimes she would phone me, begging me to return to her as quickly as possible, as the devil was with her. When I reached her she would be sitting on her bed white and shaking. I would take her in my arms and together we would pray. Slowly she would calm down and feel strong enough to resist the need to binge. Or she would phone Sister Marie McLoughlin, a dear friend and former teacher of Catherine's, and Marie would pray with Catherine over the phone. Of course, there were many times when Catherine was completely unable to resist this 'monster', and when this happened her despair and self-loathing was frightening to witness. Eventually, Catherine was able to cope with this 'devil' herself, due very much to the strength and courage that Marie was able to give her, through prayer.

Here Marie describes her first visit to Catherine at St Antony's hospital:

We drew up in the car-park of the hospital, and Hugo, Catherine's devoted golden retriever, was taken to sit on the grass outside the ground-floor window, through which he could see Catherine. We had to be careful to keep the window shut, because, on a previous occasion, he had just taken one great leap through it, and landed at the foot of her bed! Then we went in. Catherine looked like a skeleton with yellow skin stretched over it, but her hair was still beautiful, and her eyes, though sunken in, still deep and gentle. Maureen and Anna kissed her warmly and she started speaking at once, in a high voice which was almost a whisper, about some visitors who had come without asking first: she was very upset and it took Maureen some time to calm her. She was sitting on one side of the bed, with her mother next to her; I was standing on the other side waiting – she hardly noticed me. This gave me a moment to cope with myself; the shock lay not only in her personal appearance, but in the strangeness of being so near to unnatural death. 'I have a pain in my heart, here,' said Catherine, pressing her thin body. 'There is a hole in my heart.' She explained that she felt warmed by her mother's and sister's love while they were with her, but that as soon as they left to go home, the love all ran out through the hole, and a terrible desolation took hold of her. Catherine had still hardly noticed me, but I came in at this point. 'May I put my arms around you,' I said, and, in reply, she let her poor thin frame fall against me with all the confidence of a baby.

'We'll ask Jesus to fill up the hole,' was all I said. I must have held her in my arms for about half an hour, no one saying anything, except I prayed under my breath in tongues, Maureen and Anna praying with me. All was very quiet, until Catherine put the question that her family had known was coming, and that I also was to become familiar with in the time that lay ahead. 'Sister, do you think Jesus will come for me soon?'

It appeared that her mind was always turning on the thought of her death, longing for nothing else, and tormented from time to time with fits of despair because she found herself still alive. 'I don't know the answer to that,' I said. Then, after we had chatted for a little while, we left and drove home. But the next day Catherine told her mother, 'The hole in my heart is healed up'; so she was now able to retain an awareness of the love she was being given. A tiny glimmer of happiness had entered her life.

About a week after my first visit to Cheam, Catherine asked for me again. Fortunately, I managed to make myself free when she wanted me, for I knew what an effort it called for from her. Physically, yes, but even more psychologically, something had told her to control everything and everyone, and then she would 'be safe' or 'win' or whatever she needed, I don't know what it was. She had to force herself to ask me and also to demand that I come. But at this stage I decided to accept this domination completely. This, along with her other anorectic compulsions, was a way of keeping her head above water; she was fighting as hard as she could. Besides, I was afraid she might reject me if I challenged her. On this occasion she asked me, 'Sister, have you ever had morphine? You know the lovely feeling of drifting away and just leaving it all behind you ...' She longed for oblivion.

Some days later, I asked Maureen if she thought Catherine needed healing from anger. She mentioned what I had said to Catherine, who was puzzled because she did not feel angry at all. 'It stands to reason,' I said; 'Look at your situation here. You wouldn't be human if you didn't feel *some* anger about it.' There she was lying alone in a semi-dark room; outside, just a couple of yards away, were the young people, sauntering up and down in the sunshine, laughing and eating ice-cream. It made *me* angry even to think of her being deprived of such simple enjoyment, never mind all the greater pleasures and pains of life. That night there was a dramatic development. Once visitors and nurses had left her, 'all hell broke loose', as she put it, in her little room. She sensed the power of evil, an intense and violent power of anger, which threatened to engulf her. Beside herself with terror, she reached for the phone at her bedside and got through to me. 'Sister, the devil is here.' 'What is it like?' As she told me, I sensed, with her, the reality of a malignant force. So I directed a command to leave against this force, with great energy and concentration of prayer, for about half a minute, than asked Catherine how she felt, then prayed again very gently in tongues, then talked, then prayed, until she reported that this force had quite gone and she felt calm and almost asleep. It must have been an hour later that I hung up.

This sort of outburst was repeated several times in the next few days, but now Catherine had the courage to deal with it herself, and she won every time. But after such battles she needed prayer for healing in that area in herself which had been open to attack, and this was always done for her by her mother.

Perhaps some readers will find themselves translating what I have related here into other terms; since it is well known that anorectics suffer from suppressed anger, it could be said that Catherine's real anger had been allowed to surface because her mother had talked to her about it, thus communicating to her that her anger would be acceptable. She would be able to express it without any loss of love from the one person on whom she depended for life, and in this way she would be freed from it. With this explanation, the idea of evil as external to human beings but able to influence them would be removed.

During the course of Catherine's long stay in St Antony's hospital Katie Hughes, a childhood friend of hers, was

above Catherine,
aged two and a half

top right
Summer 1966: (left to right)
Anna, twenty-one months,
Catherine, four and a half,
Richard, six, and Simon, seven

right Catherine (right)
aged fifteen, with a friend

hoped into a state the whole time. GOD DAMN IT I'M HUMAN & HELPLESS WITH IT.

JUST HELP I CANNOT GO ON AWAY FROM MUMMY, SAVE ME, HELP I HAVE FEELINGS JUST LIKE ANNA. MUMMY YOU ARE MY SAVIOUR MY LIFE I CANNOT LIVE WITHOUT YOU. You have to try to understand this I cannot possibly live like this away from you. Help

mummy, I feel so awful after bingeing last night I weigh one kilo more today. Oh where am I wanted, where can I go where I will feel secure if I can't go home? I think Anna should just have to accept me, for surely I have the right to be at home, if she chooses to give up because of me then I cannot help that. I am who I am. She is intelligent and strong willed, surely she can try to be logic but she just seems to work

Pages from Catherine's diary

top left Summer 1980: (left to right) Anna, John and Catherine, eighteen and a half, weighing five stone

bottom left Catherine and Richard at Simon's wedding, 1982

above Catherine
and Richard,
February 1983

right Catherine with
her father and brothers
in December 1983,
one week before
her death

admitted for back surgery. The friendship between the two girls deepened. Katie was a source of much love and support to Catherine right to the end. She described to me how, when she had to lie flat on her back after the operation, Catherine would visit her. She would arrive late in the evening, sometimes with nothing much to say, but at other times they would talk and Catherine's anger would come flooding out. Then there were times when they would lie together on Katie's bed and Catherine would cry, without saying anything. Katie believed that Catherine saw herself as the black spot on the beauty of her family.

By the end of August, Catherine had been in hospital for over four and a half months, and I found I was in conflict with myself about whether or not to bring her home. The family was adamant that she should stay in hospital. If another emergency occurred, then everything was at hand to save her. Surely though, she would die unless she received treatment, and this she was still refusing to accept. Indeed, she frequently implored me to take her home, promising to eat if I did. Slowly, she appeared to be regaining her desire to live, but only very slowly; the compulsive urge to binge had now left her, but all the other obsessions remained very strong within her. The actual intake of food was virtually nil. Her nourishment came from the juices of the solid food which she only chewed but never swallowed. She suddenly developed an obsessive liking for grapes and melons, which lasted until her death.

In September, John had to attend a conference in America. We decided that I would go too and that we would take a few days' holiday as well. We made our arrangements so that the hospital or family could contact us easily. I had now made up my mind to bring Catherine home on our return, but in order to have the energy and strength to do this I needed a complete change. The knowledge that she was at last to come home, I knew, would give Catherine the necessary goal to look forward to, though she was distraught at the prospect of me being away for two weeks.

The previous December Anna had left the convent boarding-school; with Catherine so ill she decided she wanted to be at home, and had enrolled at a local sixth-form college. Anna wanted to read medicine, if possible at the same medical school as Simon. Her subjects were chemistry, biology and Spanish. She was advised to drop Spanish and replace it with physics if she wanted to have the best chance of obtaining a place. This meant that she had under a year to do the A-level physics course.

While we were away at the beginning of her final A-level year, she visited Catherine every day. Catherine was in a deeply distressed state and constantly making impossible demands on Anna. As well as managing Catherine patiently and well, she would do all Catherine's washing, which was heavily soiled because of her incontinence. Anna also took it upon herself to visit her grandmother once a week, in a nursing home in north London, an hour and a half's journey away through heavy traffic. The pressure on her must have been enormous, though Simon, Jenny and Richard did all they could to help and support her.

Joëlle, a friend of mine, went to the hospital late one evening, in answer to a phone call from Catherine. She felt shattered by the visit, as she told me months afterwards, for Catherine had let down all her defences in her need for help and as Joëlle expressed it, 'my inability to give her that help upset me beyond words . . . from that day onwards, I could never think of Catherine without a feeling of physical pain'.

While we were in California, we returned to the hotel

one day to find an urgent message to phone the hospital awaiting us. I was sure Catherine must have died and I couldn't make the call. With a pounding heart I shut myself in the bathroom and waited for John to get through and discover the worst. However, the call had been made by Catherine herself. Sobbing uncontrollably, she begged me to return immediately. Despite everyone's kindness and patience she couldn't manage without me, couldn't stay another day in hospital. John took the phone from me and told Catherine I would be returning on 26 September as planned and not before. Although my instinct was to rush back to England to Catherine, I knew John was right to insist that we complete our holiday together.

SIX

After six full months in hospital Catherine returned home on 1 October 1982. No one who saw her leave the hospital that day thought she would live for any length of time. She weighed less than three stone, she looked and was just a living skeleton. She was incontinent, had lost all muscle control and could only stand when supported, but none the less she wanted to live. Before leaving her hospital room she said, 'We are going to do it together.'

The one condition I made before agreeing to bring Catherine home was that she handed over her responsibility for eating to me. I wasn't at all sure that she would abide by this. She also agreed that it would be a good idea for me to sit with her during mealtimes. I made no mention of weight target, for my overwhelming desire was that she should increase her weight sufficiently to prevent her death. I started off by giving her baby food, only insisting that she swallow just one teaspoonful – and my joy when she succeeded in actually swallowing was intense, though I always tried to remain outwardly calm! However, I never stinted my praise when I felt she had done particularly well. After a few days I introduced freshly cooked food which I had prepared for the family. This she found much harder to accept. When she had difficulty in swallowing I would ask. 'Why can't you swallow, what is it that is preventing you from allowing the food to do you good?' She would reply, 'I wish I knew the answer to that.' She always completed her meal with a slice of melon and a half a pound of grapes, which she never even attempted to swallow. Her liquid intake was about one pint a day and consisted of low-calorie lemon squash and black tea. Even though her food consumption was very small, she was beginning to look noticeably better.

Remembering those weeks when I was trying to nurse Catherine back to some sort of health is like remembering a nightmare. The frights we had are too numerous to mention. As Catherine began to feel stronger she would attempt to do more and more for herself; invariably her attempts ended with her fainting or suffering a painful fall. Several times, on finding her in a faint on the floor, I believed her to be dead; on at least two occasions Anna was the one to discover her lying on the floor, and then she too suffered the shock of believing Catherine had died.

The seventeenth of October was Catherine's twenty-first birthday. Most of Catherine's friends of her own age were either away at university or abroad. Nevertheless, we decided to give her a small surprise lunchtime party. We invited friends who had known her for many years and for whom she had a special affection. She remained in bed in her room throughout, but in ones and twos everyone went upstairs to wish her 'Happy Birthday' and leave some small gift for her. She was very deeply touched and overwhelmed by the love shown to her, as were we. The support and friendship of people who went out of their way to help and understand was a constant source of strength to me.

On the morning of her birthday, I persuaded her to let me take two Instamatic photographs, one of her naked back view and the other of her head and shoulders. I hoped to shock her into seeing how she really looked. Three weeks later she asked me to take two more identical photographs.

These showed an improvement in her appearance, but she did not make any comment.

About this time I introduced Complan into Catherine's diet. I would mix Complan, dried milk, three raw eggs, natural yoghurt and ice-cream together like a thick milk-shake, about two pints in all. She would only drink this when alone, however, which made me suspicious; it wasn't long before I discovered she was disposing of at least one and a half pints of the mixture in a variety of ways. For instance, I noticed that the plants beneath her bedroom window had taken on a new creamy colouring. Another time I discovered an ornate wooden box under her bedclothes; previously she had used it for bits and bobs, now it contained the Complan mixture! When I made these discoveries I would face her with them. Sometimes she would be extremely angry, but always her anger would turn to apology and she would beg me to forgive her. I insisted there was nothing to forgive, for she was hurting only herself. If she didn't want the Complan then I wouldn't make it any more. In actual fact, I didn't worry too much that only a quarter of what I made was being consumed by Catherine – I knew that even half a pint a day of the highly nutritious drink was a very useful addition to her diet.

During this time her friend Katie Hughes came to see Catherine and after lunch I drove them to see *Rocky III* at the local cinema. It was Catherine's first outing for many months and I must admit I was more than a little apprehensive. Katie said, 'Everything she did seemed to take an eternal amount of time and energy. Climbing the steps to the ticket office become a long toil. I hardly remember the film, since I spent the whole time watching Catherine. At one point, she dropped her ticket on the floor and tried to reach for it. For an agonizing moment I believed she had collapsed and died. At the end of the afternoon I was exhausted.'

Nine weeks after her release from hospital Catherine weighed five stone, a weight gain of over two stone. Family and friends were delighted. I suppose it must have seemed like a miracle, for the living skeleton that had returned home from the hospital was indeed transformed. Though still very thin and frail-looking, she had recovered her muscle control and much of her strength, and her mental energy and concentration had also returned. Since coming home from hospital Dr Foot had attended her regularly, building on the trust Catherine had placed in her.

Catherine was now eager to find herself a job, but she decided not to go back to secretarial work; to be with children, she felt, might be the best way of helping herself. She had also a strong notion that should she get completely well she would like to become a nurse, so in her view becoming a nanny was a step in the right direction. She started to scan advertisements in the *Lady* and attended a couple of interviews at agencies. Several jobs came up and I drove her to interviews. I remember the first one clearly. I sat in the car watching her climb the five or six steps to the front door, my heart in my mouth; she appeared so shaky I thought she would fall. She told me afterwards that she too had been fearful she wouldn't manage those steps. Usually during the interview she would be taken upstairs to view the nursery and she would explain away her difficulty in mounting the stairs by saying she had injured her leg.

Catherine acquired a job looking after two adorable little girls, Christina, aged one year, and Sarah, who was three. Their mother was separated from her husband and out at work all day. This was excellent from Catherine's point of view, since there would be no one to bother her about whether she ate or not, and she would have every weekend at home. Catherine loved the job and became very attached to the children. Before long she had made herself virtually indispensable. As well as caring for the little girls, she would clean the three-storey terraced house from top to bottom, do all the washing and ironing and quite often the shopping as well. How she found the strength for such a physically demanding job I will never know, but that was typically Catherine! At home at the weekends she would be mentally and physically exhausted, and she would rest a great deal in order to recharge herself for the coming week.

When Catherine was offered this job I debated whether to phone the mother and tell her of Catherine's illness, thereby almost certainly losing for Catherine this opportunity to prove herself, or let Catherine go ahead and not say anything. I decided after much thought on the latter, but the mother rang me shortly after Catherine had commenced working and asked me if she had anorexia, and on learning that she had, asked me how I thought she could best help Catherine. I told her on no account to make Catherine aware that she knew, not to watch her when eating and, most important, to let Catherine feel that she had her trust and confidence.

Christmas that year was quieter than usual. For the first time in many years my sister and her family were not with us. After dinner we played the usual party games, the nativity plays having been long since outgrown! Catherine was sitting observing everything, but unable to take part. I asked her if she would like to read us a favourite poem. To my surprise she agreed. She chose 'Hunchback', a poem I was not familiar with, but which was particularly poignant because of the strong analogy between herself and the isolation of the little hunchback.

84

She returned to her job but began to find the mental strain too much. She would sometimes phone me during the day, often on the verge of breaking down. She admitted that the binging/vomiting syndrome had returned; she would yield to it at night when she could give vent to it undisturbed. As a result she was losing out on much-needed sleep and rest. The anorexia still had Catherine in its grip.

On the Saturday before our twenty-fifth wedding anniversary, John and I were encouraged to go out for the day. Catherine and Anna explained to me that they, with Simon, Jenny and Richard, had planned a small family dinner-party for us; they wanted it to be a surprise, but I had to be let in to the secret as it was my job to keep their father out all day. On our return that evening we were ushered upstairs and told to tidy up! An hour or so later we were 'invited' downstairs and offered pre-dinner sherry. We were impressed by how smart they all looked and touched that they should have gone to such trouble. As we were sitting quietly enjoying our drinks, the doorbell rang and I remember wondering who it could be at that time. It turned out to be one of the ushers at our wedding and his wife, friends we hadn't seen for some years. Within minutes more people came and the penny soon dropped! Meanwhile flower arrangements appeared and large trays holding glasses of sherry were being offered around. Catherine's eyes never left our faces as we greeted each new arrival. The party was a tremendous success; everyone had entered into the conspiracy with great enthusiasm. Friends who lived locally had not given anything away by so much as a look or word.

The idea of the party was Catherine's, and it was she who had phoned or written to all the guests. On the morning of the party Catherine and Anna had risen early and gone to the local market to buy the fresh vegetables and salad, including eighty onions! They also collected their order of 20lb of chopped beef from the butcher. With the shopping done they had set about the lengthy preparation and cooking of beef carbonnade for more than fifty people. They had also made a selection of puddings. One of these, baked by Catherine earlier in the week, was called 'Passion cake'! She had also made, with the permission of her employer, a very large and delicious fruit cake, which Anna iced on the afternoon of the party. My mother, who was with them during all the preparations of that day, told me afterwards of the pleasure she had felt at hearing so much chatter and laughter coming from the kitchen. She said, 'They didn't walk from the kitchen to the dining-room, they ran.' A friend of Anna's had advised them on the choice of wine, and champagne was provided to accompany the anniversary cake. Throughout the evening Catherine was at our side watching us, as if she was basking in our pleasure.

By the early hours of the morning all our guests had left and Catherine, looking pale and exhausted, went to bed. John, Simon, Jenny, Richard, Anna and I stayed up talking. I told them that the party had been an important challenge to Catherine, the reason she had been able to keep going, and that the next day she would be deeply depressed.

Simon and Jenny left by mid-morning. They were working hard for their finals in June and wanted to return to their books. As expected, a black depression had descended on Catherine, so black she couldn't even speak. She stayed in bed. John and I had been invited by friends for lunchtime drinks and left about 12.40, leaving Anna studying in her bedroom and Richard reading the newspaper in the kitchen.

We had been with our friends only minutes when the phone rang – Catherine had collapsed.

We rushed home, Dr Foot arriving seconds after we did. Catherine had taken an overdose. I travelled with Catherine in the ambulance that rushed us to the hospital, with John and Anna following in the car. All I remember about the journey is talking to Catherine, something telling me that I mustn't let her sleep. On arrival she was taken immediately to have the contents of her stomach pumped out. We stayed with Catherine for four or five hours.

Apparently, after we left for the drinks party Catherine had come downstairs and made herself a cup of coffee. She was sitting on a stool at the kitchen counter, when her head suddenly dropped forward on to the counter. Richard reached her just in time to prevent her hitting the floor. He shouted for Anna and together they carried her upstairs and laid her on the bed. Anna, having raised her legs and put her head on one side, dashed to the phone and rang Dr Foot and us. Catherine told me afterwards that the tablets had acted faster than she anticipated. She thought they would take at least half an hour to work, so she had decided to have a coffee and be back in bed by the time the tablets started to take effect.

At half-past ten that night the phone rang. It was the hospital. Catherine was insisting on discharging herself. On reaching the hospital we and the sister-in-charge said everything we could think of to dissuade her from coming home. It proved useless. As I've said before, arguing with an anorectic is futile. A young woman doctor arrived on the scene. While I stayed with Catherine, she saw John and proceeded to give him a good talking to about wanting to take his daughter, in her poor condition, out of hospital.

John managed to interrupt, 'Excuse me, I don't believe you have the correct story ...'

For some days afterwards Catherine remained in bed at home, sleeping a great deal. She would come downstairs only to prepare her meagre meal and then disappear with it back to her room. Whenever possible I sat with her and when she was able to we talked. Her deep desire to die was back – she could no longer face life. She constantly needed me to enfold her in my arms. I rang the mother of the two little girls and told her that Catherine would not be returning.

One afternoon, during one of our talks, Catherine asked, 'Do you know why I stopped eating so suddenly at the beginning?', I replied, 'No,' though I believed I knew the answer. However, I wasn't prepared for her reply. 'To protect you; you see,' she went on to explain, 'the only way I could make myself ill was to stop eating and the only way I would be allowed home was for me to become ill. I was so frightened about you being alone with Daddy.'

John and I had planned a week's visit to Israel to mark our twenty-fifth wedding anniversary and we were undecided whether to go or not. The family, including Catherine, insisted that we should, and at the last minute we decided to go ahead with the planned holiday.

Our week in the Holy Land was both a deeply spiritual and visually fascinating experience for me. At every opportunity I raised my dearest daughter Catherine up to God, praying for her suffering and anguish to end, for her to be healed and find peace within herself. For me the holiday became a pilgrimage on Catherine's behalf.

Richard met us on our return to Gatwick Airport. All was well, he told us. Much later that evening we heard about Catherine's second attempt to take her life, only the previous night. I sensed a desperation in Anna, indeed we all felt it. I rang Dr Foot and asked if she knew a qualified doctor who would give Catherine hypnotherapy. She found one and within two days he came to see us.

I suppose we had all pinned our hopes on this psychiatrist, but sadly the much needed help wasn't forthcoming. This proved too much for Anna. She had seen so much of her sister's suffering, and now her sister had made two attempts to kill herself. She could not imagine the depths of despair that made Catherine want to end her life so desperately.

Here Anna describes an incident that took place between them.

The first suicide attempt had been a big enough shock to me but when there was a second one, I really did not think I could cope. I felt I was going to snap into pieces. It was this second suicide attempt that made me realize how great Catherine's addiction to hoarding tablets was. She had a whole briefcase full. I struggled to snatch the case, but Catherine's grip on it was so strong I could not take it from her, even using two hands. Her desperate look, her screaming and her addiction haunted me. I felt I was looking at someone I had never seen before. This girl was not Catherine. I couldn't believe that someone could alter so much, fall so very low, especially Catherine. I think the love I felt for her emerged as hurt and depression for quite a while.

When the psychiatrist left the house Anna begged Catherine to go to hospital and accept treatment. Catherine said she couldn't. At Catherine's refusal to go to hospital Anna's sobs became uncontrollable. Between sobs she told us she could no longer work, she was giving everything up. Anna's desperation and despair prompted John to phone Dr Foot, who came immediately. Seeing Anna crouched on the floor, she sat on the floor too and put her arms around her. I don't remember all she said but I do remember her saying, 'You don't feel you can cope now, but I can assure you in a couple of weeks you will feel differently. Anna, people who haven't known suffering make rotten doctors – you will make a wonderful doctor.' Before leaving she gave me something for Anna that made her sleep soundly for twelve hours. It was almost three months before Anna was able to give full concentration and effort to her A-level studies again.

On the following day Catherine packed her cases and set off to stay with her grandmother; on arriving, she told my mother she would like to stay with her for some time, and that she would find a job locally. 'I will look after you, Granny,' she added. When I drove to my mother's home the following morning, she was very relieved to see me. She had been very alarmed by Catherine's appearance – Catherine's weight was now four and a half stone and she looked gaunt and hollow-eyed. Catherine, however, showed no emotion at seeing me, indeed, she appeared not to notice my arrival.

I intended to stay at my mother's with Catherine for as long as it took to persuade Catherine to accept hospitalization, which I felt was imperative, as much for Anna's well-being as for Catherine's. Late on Sunday evening Catherine told me she would go into hospital, but only for a rest; she adamantly refused to receive any treatment. Dr Foot then rang numerous hospitals, but none would accept Catherine without her agreeing to be treated. John contacted the doctor who had given Catherine psychotherapy in 1979, and he recommended a well-known professor. Speaking to the professor, Dr Foot learned that he had twenty cases a week like Catherine referred to him and he could only accept one; the soonest he could give her an appointment would be in July and there would not be a bed available in his unit until the following November, another eight months!

After two days of telephone calls, Dr Foot finally arranged

for Catherine to go into a private psychiatric hospital in Roehampton. The consultant who was to look after her decided that Catherine's only chance was in having compulsory treatment and so on 2 March 1983 I drove Catherine to the hospital from my mother's home. She had no idea that she would be placed once again under Section 26 of the Mental Health Act. Personally, I do not believe that sectioning an anorectic is any answer at all, unless he or she wishes it. I knew from past experience that sectioning Catherine had led to her distrust of doctors and hospitals and to her refusing to receive any help after her eighteenth birthday for fear of being sectioned. At this point, though, I was so desperate that I knew I had to allow it for all our sakes. During the two days I had spent with her at my mother's she had been very ill, and with her routine broken she was unable to cope mentally.

'Never at any stage did I expect her to recover,' Dr Foot commented to me later. 'There was an inevitability about the way she tackled non-eating, binging, eating vast quantities of Senokot and hiding food.' (Catherine would obtain the Senokot, a laxative, by telephoning the chemist, usually a different one each time, and ordering one or more tins, each containing one thousand tablets.) Initially to her, 'Catherine was a strong personality who just happened to use anorexia nervosa as a disease in order to die with a clear conscience ... she had no fear of death but did get very distressed by disturbance in vision, angina-like pains and headache resulting from her extreme weakness.' Just before Catherine died, she gave Dr Foot a small jewellery box for Christmas. 'It reminds me daily of the bond we formed – as partners. As a GP she managed me. Oh yes – she managed me successfully,' she added.

The night before I arrived at my mother's, Catherine had phoned Marie, who had helped her so much during her lengthy stay in hospital the previous year, and in a very distressed and desperate state had asked Marie to pray with her. She was suicidal and begging Marie for help. Over the phone Marie talked to her and prayed, and then gently told her to give any tablets she might have to her grandmother. When she had done this she asked Catherine to phone back. Catherine did not hand over the tablets. Despite her despairing mental condition, she would not have wanted to frighten her grandmother. I believe she flushed the tablets (if she had any at the time) down the lavatory, because I found no trace of any except Senokot when I unpacked for her at the hospital three days later.

Catherine's Diary

26 February 1983

Right now, I feel lost, lonely and frightened. I cannot cope with my binging here. I cannot stay, my anorexia takes even more of a hold on me when away from Mummy. I will not accept any form of treatment, but I do know for certain that without Mummy I am just totally unable to cope. I realize the situation at home but I feel that Anna is being a little hard on me. I have to come home to live right now. I just don't know what will happen to me. I love my father and all my family but I need even more my mother. I need her to keep me as sane as I will ever be. I have so much hidden inside myself, I need to be near her, WITH HER. Is that fair? I ask myself. Well at this moment in time, I just know that I need her more so than even Anna. Anna is strong, intelligent and sensible, but me, I have no confidence and am just a little helpless baby. All I can do is cry and cry Help me, save me, help me please. At least Mummy rescue me. I know what its like when Anna and I are together but right now I am in pieces. I dread and fear Daddy's reaction, his fury, frustration and anger because of my inability to be away from Mummy. But sometimes Anna has got to be made to understand. I know that I couldn't even go to Margaret alone. I could fill this whole book with talk. But basically it is all a vicious circle. I need my mother, my home, my room and all my things to keep me alive. I can no longer eat anything just drink coffee, bovril and suck lemon ice cubes. It is not a threat but I am so choked I just cannot carry on. I will never be able to work again. I shall just be a lonesome invalid who lives in her world, with room for my mother. I just don't know where to turn or what to do or say. God please take me. Having to go away and be away has made me realize just exactly who and what I am. Hard, it may seem to believe, but believe me it has cut me up completely.

The following morning

This morning I feel so frightened and alone, I just want to sit and cry. I need my home and Mummy. Oh God where do I go? I cannot face up to it, life I mean like this. I need my home, my room, my family, but more than anything in this world I need Mummy. I feel so awful after binging last night. I weigh one kilo more today. Oh where am I wanted, where can I go where I will feel secure if I can't go home? I think Anna should have to accept me, for surely I have the right to be at home. If she chooses to give up because of me then I cannot help that. I am who I am. She is intelligent and strong willed, surely she can try to be logical but she just seems to work herself into a state.

GOD IM HUMAN AND HELPLESS
JUST HELP I CANNOT GO ON
AWAY FROM MUMMY SAVE ME, HELP
MUMMY YOU ARE MY SAVIOUR MY LIFE
I CANNOT LIVE WITHOUT YOU.

You have to see and understand this. I cannot possibly live like this away from you. Help please help say you want me.
I know I am a burden, trouble, a pain. But the pain which is

93

going through me all the time is just too great to explain. All I know is it hurts. Please stay with me, help me. Just being with you, knowing you are always by my side is what helps me. It may not seem that way, but yesterday and the past few days have all been too great. No one has really thought of some way to a solution because it is a question of just getting me away but you can't just do that, I can't take it. I just can't. I wish I could explain how I feel but nothing I say is ever taken seriously, it is always one big vicious circle.

'Since 18 you have had your own way' TRUE TRUE but no one can make me better – I just need love and Mummy. I love Daddy too very very much, don't think that I don't, but everyone is different. Help me, be near me by me stand with me. The agony I am in is too great. I wish for all our sakes God would take me. That is why I am now on a total starvation diet. In fact I am so choked up and filled with pain that I don't even feel like eating. But then at night when I am scared and alone I binge because of the thought of being without Mummy and home.

It is a way of trying to numb my pain and torture myself. Oh I don't know where to stop. Hurry, hurry, take me in your arms and never let me go. Please never let me go. I will die I am cut into pieces so small that I can never put them together again. Oh if only you and Anna could understand this, if I could, if Daddy, Simon, Richard, Jenny or anyone could. I am just a baby. I can't live or fend for myself by myself.

HELP

COME TO ME PLEASE

Every car I hear I hope it is you but time drags and I am so scared that you won't come.

Daddy Mummy the world there is no solution to my problem. Just I need home and you. You cannot just write me off until June or for a minute. If you didn't want me why did you bring me into this world.

I am on a knife's edge and can't help any more.

This is no business problem but a problem (what sort you would call it I don't know).

Oh are you coming to help me, I am just like a new-born infant but with more feeling and fear and loneliness.

HELP   HELP   HELP

Stay with me help
me please help
stay, stay, stay hold
me show me you love
me despite my horrid personality and
what I appear to be.
But I am alive and Oh God here goes
what more can I say it just goes
on and on. It never ends Take me
I would rather you killed me than leave me
I seriously mean it. Stay with me
take me back to my home
my land of living I cannot cope with different
places

HELP   PLEASE   PLEASE

take me. I'm alone so alone I am not
normal I am odd so it is so easy for you
to say a day or two won't give it a try
but for me it is a lifetime of misery
and every second is at least a year. Come
Come my God don't think that I don't
care about Anna because I do very much
and even now if she fails I shall be at
fault and carry that burden too
But I am just being destroyed we have
to find a solution you cannot just say
do this you're going there, it's tough
because it isn't right I'm not able
to really explain how I feel because there is

no way in which I can do so.
It's easy for you humans to be logical
and try to explain that what is happening
is right because I am so odd

Call it what you like. But help please
please just help me.

RIGHT NOW Take me home, let's take
it from there but I cannot stay here away
from you.

SEVEN

On arrival at the hospital Catherine decided she would not stay. The doctor who was to admit her talked to her and tried very hard to persuade her to remain voluntarily. When she refused he said, 'You cannot go home, Catherine, you have to stay here, you have been sectioned.' With this news I could see she was trying desperately to retain her equilibrium; the shock to her was enormous. She demanded to know who had been responsible, and John replied that he was the one who had insisted upon sectioning. He made no mention that I had known about it, or that Dr Foot had had to play a part in it. It had been agreed that it was of the utmost importance that Catherine's trust in both Dr Foot and myself should not be destroyed. All the old animosity Catherine had felt for her father in the past came to the fore. It was several weeks before she could bear to speak to him.

Finally she asked to be alone with me in her room. All her panic and fear became evident. She insisted she would not cooperate and she begged me not to leave her. When the doctor returned she refused to allow him to examine her. A nurse entered with a syringe and very quickly, before she had time to object, the doctor put the needle in to her arm. Within two or three minutes she was oblivious to everything; he nodded to me to leave. Afterwards he told me that her physical condition was very poor. She was given constant nursing round the clock for several days. It was two weeks before I was allowed to visit Catherine.

When I saw Catherine again she weighed six stone, her face was bloated and her beautiful thick hair, which had suffered the effects of anorexia so badly, looked thinner and in poorer condition than before. To everyone in the hospital she seemed to be cooperating, she was helpful and she was doing well. It was the old story, she was cooperating in order to get out and so be able to starve herself again, but she had been sectioned for one year and so uppermost in her mind was the need to be free; she was already planning to appeal against her sectioning. About this time the consultant had to go away, and left Catherine in the care of a colleague. She quickly developed a rapport with this doctor and, most important, she felt she could trust him. In eight weeks she reached her normal weight of 7st 8lb but her torment, anguish and conflict was, if anything, worse. She told me not to fear that she would take her own life for, as she phrased it, 'If I die now you wouldn't be burying the real me.' She hated herself. The new weight had gone on all over but it was explained to me, when someone as emaciated as Catherine was putting on weight it goes on in much the same way as a baby's, hence the fat tummy and plump face. Her new hair was also soft and fine like a young child's hair.

While Catherine was under this doctor he saw John and me regularly, and with great clarity and patience at last helped us to understand anorexia. He said, 'It isn't like measles that comes and goes, it becomes an integral part of the person and that is why it is so dangerous.' He went on to say that breaking free from anorexia was as bad, if not worse, than coming off heroin. He told us that though Catherine was twenty-one, much of her was still like a thirteen-year-old, and should she manage to maintain her normal weight, then she would go through a phase of adolescence, the adolescence which, because of her illness, she had never had.

During her stay at this hospital Catherine refused to see anyone except me and, in the latter weeks, her father – this mainly because we were now seeing the doctor regularly, with Catherine participating with us in our discussions. Her refusal to see anyone, even her brothers and sister, was because she simply could not bear to be seen as she said, 'so ugly and fat'. I believe that had she been allowed to see visitors from the start, she would not have needed to 'hide away' from all contact with family and friends. Also had her target weight not been so high, then the ordeal for her of putting on weight might not have been so traumatic. Although I fully realize that for the chronically anorectic it is essential that weight is put on, I do think that during treatment less emphasis should be placed on weight gain.

Two weeks before she was discharged, Catherine set about looking for another job as a nanny. Her fear of coming home and facing people's reaction to how she looked was immense, so to live away and yet close enough for me to visit her was, she felt, the ideal answer to her problem. She was fortunate in finding a family with two little boys aged four and seven, who lived only two miles away from us. The mother knew of her anorexia – a friend of hers had taught Catherine at school – but Catherine was unaware of this. She did her job well and became very fond of the family.

Catherine still had to see her doctor at the hospital once a week. She had been told by him that if she managed to maintain her weight at 7st 8lb for three months, then he would consider releasing her from sectioning. To be released, to be free of doctors, was the thought which preoccupied her totally. When working it was always there in her mind, when not working it obsessed her. I would visit her almost every evening and on her days and weekends off we would go out together. On these occasions she would unburden herself by talking freely about her feelings and attitudes, particularly her attitudes to life and death. Even a few hours spent with Catherine, talking against what I considered then to be her negativism, was a draining and exhausting experience. To her doctor she would talk of her plans for the future, returning home, going back to secretarial work, etc. To me she would speak of her longing to opt out of life, her fear of relationships and most of all the dark desire within her to go back into starvation. Catherine trusted me implicitly and therefore felt completely safe in talking to me as she did. I, on the other hand, was torn in two. I knew that alone I was unable to help her fight the anorexia. I could show her patience, give her love and all the support she needed, but the anorexia was bigger than both of us. I decided that if she was to have any chance of life at all, I had to break that trust. I decided to confide everything she had said to me in confidence to her doctor.

He showed no surprise, for he had fathomed Catherine weeks before and had treated enough anorectics to know how their minds work. Shortly after I had disclosed all Catherine's genuine thoughts and feelings to him, he asked me if I would be prepared to confront Catherine with them in front of him. I was aghast, I told him I couldn't do it to her, I couldn't betray Catherine in front of him. I was fearful of her reaction – not just her possible hatred of me as a consequence, but the very real risk of her suicide. He suggested I think it over and telephone him when I had made a decision. I discussed it with Simon, Richard and Anna; they felt as I did that it would break Catherine and destroy for her the one strong and secure relationship which they felt was vital to her. John, however, felt it was worth taking the risk; as nothing had worked for her, we had to take this last chance.

I rang the doctor and told him I couldn't do it. He explained his aim, which was to show Catherine how much I hated the anorexia, but loved *her*. He wanted to separate my love for Catherine from her anorexia. He said, 'She will probably hate you, but not for long. Young children never hate their parents because they are too dependent on them. Because Catherine is so dependent on you, she won't be able to hate you.' We talked at length and I said I would try and do as he wished. He explained that he would prompt me during the session, but if I felt unable to confront Catherine then he would not pursue it, he would respect my feelings. I came to realize that my love for Catherine was greater than any breakdown in our relationship; if she hated me, if she never wanted to see me again but gained some control over the anorexia, then this confrontation would have been well worth it in every possible way.

A few days after my telephone conversation with the doctor I drove Catherine to the hospital; she was always in a state of turmoil before the sessions, dreading that he would find out that she had lost weight. She would go to great lengths to keep her weight loss from the nurse who weighed her, hiding paperweights in her clothing, wearing extra clothes and drinking several cups of black coffee before I collected her. On her previous visit it had been discovered what she was doing and as a result he had put back her release from section by one week. She had been thrown into a greater state of panic than usual. On these journeys to the hospital I would spend the time trying to calm her and reason with her. This particular morning I was the one who needed reassurance. Inside, I was in turmoil and in fear and trepidation of the outcome of what I was about to do.

We were met by the doctor immediately on arrival and as usual the discussion started in as relaxed an atmosphere as possible. After the opening preliminaries he told Catherine that he believed she would go back into starvation when he discharged her. I knew this was my cue, but I kept quiet – I couldn't say anything. After several such cues I finally found the courage and went ahead and faced Catherine with everything she had ever said to me in confidence. If looks could have killed I would not be sitting here now writing this! Catherine was devastated. Although outwardly she was fighting to keep calm in front of the doctor, underneath I could sense her feelings of betrayal, her anger, and her total lack of understanding as to why I was doing this to her. She admitted everything I had said was the truth, and for a while entered into a discussion with him. Finally, he asked, 'Why do you think your mother has done this, Catherine?' Suddenly, all the terrible hurt feelings she had been trying to keep submerged erupted and she ran from the room. Shortly afterwards I went back to where the car was parked, hoping and dreading at the same time to find Catherine there. She wasn't. The doctor came out to go to his car; when he saw Catherine wasn't with me he went back into the hospital to search for her. I remained where I was in case she appeared. She was not to be found anywhere. He felt sure, he told me, that Catherine would make her way back; my best plan was to go home for he felt certain Catherine would contact me. I decided to drive around the locality first in the hope of spotting her. I was almost giving up when, for some reason, I drove to the nearest high street, perhaps twenty minutes' walk from the hospital, and parked my car in one of the side roads. Walking along past the shops I suddenly heard

Catherine's voice shout, 'Mummy'. I turned, only to receive a sharp ringing slap across the face, and loud, angry abuse and accusations. Before I could recover from the shock she had run off again. I found her minutes later crouched sobbing behind a telephone booth in a turning off the main street. It took all my strength to appear firm and calm; she lashed out at me once again. I grabbed her arms and told her that if she did not return to the car with me, I would leave her there. We returned to the car and once inside she turned on me again. I tried to explain that my feelings for her were as they had always been, that it was her anorexia, the thing that had such a hold on her, that I loathed and hated.

As we were driving along she started to speak about how she felt: what I had done was unthinkable, how could the mother she so loved and trusted betray her? Suddenly, while going along an open stretch of road, she opened her door and for one terrifying moment I thought she was going to throw herself from the car. I slowed down for her to close the door. For the rest of the journey I drove slowly and in silence.

When we reached the house of the family where she worked, she got out of the car. As she walked through the garden gate she turned and said, in a hard, loud voice, 'I never want to see you again.'

After a couple of hours spent in a café drinking black coffee, I felt able to go home, only to find that Catherine had been constantly phoning and wanting me. Anna had prepared the meal. She said, 'I knew it would be an especially difficult day for you, so I went ahead.' I was so grateful for her thoughtfulness.

Fearing Catherine's state of mind, I went straight to her. I found her preparing the children's supper. Their parents had gone out for the evening. I went into the little flat which she occupied on the ground floor. Once she had the children settled in front of the television watching a favourite programme and eating their meal, she came to me. She closed the door and for a moment said nothing. Then all her enraged and furious feelings came to the fore. She was baffled and bewildered by my betrayal. I had never seen such fierce passion, such wild anger in Catherine. At the height of her hysteria she began to produce carrier bags from behind chairs and out of cupboards; suddenly the floor was strewn with dozens of packets of biscuits and bars of chocolate. Then all her enraged fury seemed to subside. 'This is what it's like to have anorexia,' she said. Calmly she went on to tell me how ever since she had been discharged from hospital, but was forced to keep her weight up because she had not been discharged from sectioning, she had found herself surreptitiously taking food from shops, mainly biscuits and chocolate, which she didn't like and never ate. Sometimes, she told me, she was unaware of her stealing and would be shocked to find items for which she had not paid in her bag after leaving the shop. At other times the urge to steal would come upon her while she was in the shop and she would put the items in her bag and feel a kind of elation at what she was doing. Within a short time of committing these acts she would be filled with remorse and self-loathing, filled with such disgust that she would sink into deep despair over what she had become. I had sat quietly witnessing this terrifying outburst over my 'betrayal' with feelings of overwhelming pain and sadness. I felt no shock when she told me of her shoplifting, all I said was, 'Catherine, you know what you have become – a common thief.' 'Yes, I know that,' she replied, 'I hate myself for it.' With that she came into my arms, 'Hold me, hold me,' she kept saying. I felt such love for her, yet at the same time such deep hopelessness.

In July 1983, her sectioning was brought to an end. Her doctor felt that its usefulness was over; had he not released her, then she simply would not have cooperated. I agreed, for I felt the continuing strain of it on Catherine might very well have led to another attempt on her own life. I told him that even if she went back into starvation there was always the slight hope that she might turn away from it before it was too late. 'Should she go back into starvation,' he said, 'I give her three to six months to live.'

Once free of Section 26 of the Mental Health Act, she was more relaxed than I had seen her for a long time. She wanted to return to secretarial work and use her brain once more. The family for whom she had been working as a nanny were sympathetic and understanding. She applied for jobs. To her amazement (and mine) her secretarial skills had not diminished in the least, despite her long absence from this type of work, and she must have interviewed very well, for she was offered three interesting jobs simultaneously. The one she chose involved working as secretary to two editors at the Reuter News Agency in Fleet Street.

Catherine returned home three days before she was due to start her new job in the middle of July 1983. She still could not cope with seeing any of the family or her close friends. Simon, Jenny and Richard were all working, so Catherine's not being able to face them presented no problems, and Anna was away for most of the summer, first as an au pair with friends of ours in Spain, and then in Italy staying with other friends.

While Anna was in Spain we received the wonderful news that she had achieved the A-level results which would enable her to go to medical school the following October. Catherine cried with joy at Anna's success, and told me that she would have blamed herself if Anna had not succeeded.

Catherine's mind was still a twisted agony of misconceptions about herself; she believed that she was fat, ugly and grotesque. She hated the secretiveness of her illness, and the way in which it had changed her so fundamentally and at the same time become her way of life and her security. None of this would be apparent, though, to her new work colleagues – to them I'm sure she appeared a very hard-working, conscientious but likeable young girl who wasn't particularly keen on going out for meals or drinks.

Once in her new job, Catherine established a routine from which she never deviated. She was always up by 7.45, having laid her clothes out in readiness the night before. She would drive to the station (not the local one in case she was seen by anyone she knew), and then take the train for Victoria and the tube to Blackfriars. From there she would walk to her place of work in Fleet Street, which was a long walk for Catherine. She weighed 7½st when she started and she was still doing it three months later, weighing only 4st 4lb. At night she would return home drained and exhausted. She would prepare some food for herself, occasionally accepting a little of what I had prepared, and always finished her so-called meal with the inevitable grapes and melon. After this she would take a bath and then get into bed to watch television until it closed down. She rarely slept before one in the morning. Often I would sit with her while she told me about her day – she enjoyed her work and loved to talk to me about it. On Saturdays she would rise at ten o'clock and shop for her supply of grapes and melons for the week. Afterwards she liked us to go somewhere together, sometimes the country, sometimes the coast and once London, when she surprised me by producing tickets for an evening performance at the theatre. During the last few weeks or so of her working life, apart from shopping for the fruit and cleaning her room, she would spend most of the weekend resting. In September she felt able to see the other members of the family and certain friends again; I suppose because of her dramatic weight loss she felt they would be seeing 'her' and not someone else.

People at Reuters had noticed the tremendous change in Catherine's appearance over such a short time. She worried greatly about their remarks and, even more, she worried that they would reach the conclusion that she suffered from anorexia. Her editors and the other secretaries showed obvious concern for her.

The twenty-fifth of October was to be her last day at work. That morning she had forced herself out of the house, and, despite feeling extremely ill, she somehow managed to make the journey to work. When she finally reached her office her condition must have been apparent to everyone and she was sent home by car with a welfare officer from the company. This time she had come home to die.

EIGHT

Now that her need to fight, to push herself, was over, Catherine's physical deterioration was rapid. She still insisted on cleaning and vacuuming her own room though she was becoming slower and slower. She could walk up and down stairs, but with the greatest difficulty. For the first six weeks she was home we had some happy outings together; one particularly memorable one was when we visited Sister Marie, who now lived in Oxford. Catherine so wanted to see her.

This is how Marie described that visit:

I had arranged a couch for her in the library, a large tranquil room looking out on to the University Parks, and put three late roses and some lavender in a vase on a low table near it, and a little gift wrapped up in some decorative paper. I wanted these preparations to speak for me. When the car drew up I watched Catherine get out; watched the langour of her movements and the slow articulation of her knee and hip joints as she walked to the door, supported by her mother. Then I opened it and was greeted by her slow smile and her deep eyes. Maureen helped her to the couch, and for most of the visit she lay there, while her mother talked to me, telling me all the family news that Catherine had evidently asked her to. It would have been too tiring for her to talk herself. Meanwhile, I was sitting back on my heels on the floor, holding her hand.

When the talking was finished none of us felt the need to say or do anything, so we just sat in silence, while the quiet afternoon light filled the room. Then Catherine said: 'Sister, do you think Jesus will come for me soon?'

'You know, Catherine,' I answered, 'you are holding my hand. That means you are trusting me. I think Jesus wants you to trust him, because life in heaven is a life of trusting. You are preparing for it.'

'Yes,' said Catherine with peace in her face.

When Maureen said that they must be going, I got her a cup of tea, and half a glass of hot water for Catherine into which she put a few drops of low-calorie blackcurrant juice. She took two mouthfuls. As we went out to the car, I with my arm through Catherine's, she was so light that it was like carrying a walking stick. I waved them off, and turned back, feeling that she had given me so much love simply by coming all that way in that state.

Catherine came away glowing inwardly; the peace which had been growing within her seemed to intensify that day.

Another time I drove her to the little seaside town on the east coast where my mother had lived for so long, and where Catherine had spent many happy holidays during her childhood. We visited the old haunts and it saddened me to realize that Catherine was saying goodbye to them all. I wanted to envelope her in love, to demonstrate such love that she would not want to leave us.

Catherine was very eager to visit Anna at College Hall, so one afternoon I took her. She really enjoyed seeing Anna's room and was happy that she would be able to picture her sister in her surroundings. Of that visit, Anna wrote: 'It was also very important to me, because she met my two best friends at Barts. I desperately wanted them to understand. I felt that before they knew Catherine, they did not know *me* completely. I tried to bring Catherine into the conversation numerous times, but I knew she was in her own world.'

One Sunday, while at home, Richard took Catherine out in the wheelchair. She was now too weak to walk more than a few steps without help and in order to be able to take her out as much as possible we hired a wheelchair from the Red Cross. She was dressed warmly and covered by a blanket. She looked so fragile. On returning home, I asked if they had had a nice walk. Richard answered: 'I got a little tired half way, so Catherine got out and pushed me!' I remember Catherine being highly amused at this joke. It was the first time for ages that we had seen her really laugh – and it was the last.

Her final outing in a wheelchair was to have her hair cut and to do her Christmas shopping. I will always remember the gentleness and consideration given to Catherine by the young man who cut her hair. If she had been the most glamorous model instead of the pathetic, emaciated, waif-like figure she was, he couldn't have shown more care and attention. I felt so grateful to him. She asked me to wheel her to the basement of a large department store; there she insisted on buying me two vacuum cleaners, one a turbo-jet model and the other a portable. 'I want to make things easier for you,' was how she explained her purchases. After that we concentrated on the buying of presents. She enjoyed it all. Pushing her through the shopping precinct I could hear her singing along with the Christmas carols being relayed over the loudspeakers.

The shopping expedition had not been without its traumas. On one occasion she had leant forward, lost her balance and fallen out of the wheelchair. Earlier in the day, while shopping for the vacuum cleaners, there had been a moment of crisis when I had had to rush to the ladies' room on the third floor – no easy task in a shop crowded with Christmas shoppers.

Over the weeks Catherine was visited frequently by a

young priest who had recently joined our parish. She liked Father John instantly and regarded him as a special friend. So many friends, by visiting, writing, sending flowers, tried in their own ways to instil a desire to live in Catherine, but she only wanted to die. Only God, she felt, truly understood her, and only he could release her from her suffering. 'Why hasn't he taken me?' was her constant question.

Sitting with her one afternoon, she suddenly asked, 'What am I doing wrong?' I knew what she meant – she wanted to be worthy to go to Heaven.

Another time I said, 'What do you think Heaven is like, Catherine?' She replied, 'I believe it is a place where there is great peace, joy and freedom.' She hesitated for a moment and added, 'And warmth.' After her death, I thought of this description a great deal and found comfort in the way she had said, 'And warmth.' The use of this word conjured up many things, the warmth of love, warmth of happiness, and the warmth of basking in Christ's light; I believe she meant the latter. Feeling helpless in my efforts to prevent Catherine dying I said to her, quite crossly, 'How do you think I'm going to feel when you die?' She replied, so gently and softly, 'You must not be sad, Mummy, I will be happy and therefore you must be too.' Half laughing, half crying, I said, 'Make sure you keep a place in Heaven for me.'

During the last two weeks Catherine suffered intolerable physical pain. She never once admitted this or complained. I knew, for I saw it written on her face, and while sleeping she was constantly crying out in agony.

'How do you bear this pain?' I asked one day. Her answer stunned me. 'I offer it up because of all the suffering I have caused you.' What could I say? I went downstairs and sobbed my heart out.

Catherine had been at home about two weeks when I

received a phone call from a young girl, who herself was suffering from anorexia, and who wished to visit Catherine. I knew her family slightly, as we lived in the same locality, but neither Catherine nor I had ever met Patricia. For Patricia that first sight of Catherine was both horrific and frightening. 'When I first met Catherine,' she said, 'the sight of her shocked me so much, it just blew my mind. I had never seen anything quite like it.' But once the initial shock had worn off she was able to talk for the first time to someone who understood completely all she was saying. The sense of release to Patricia was immense, and for those last weeks of Catherine's life a wonderful bond of love and understanding developed between the two girls. Below is the letter Catherine wrote and left for Patricia. Richard found it just a few hours after her death.

14 December 1983
3 a.m.

Dear Patricia,

I am writing this to you when I feel most able and right now I seem able of doing that.

It is to tell you that your life is worth living, and even if I am not there to help you, that battle for FREEDOM from anorexia will be much harder but please don't forget all that I have told you.

You are eighteen years old. You are young, no matter what you think or feel *you are* very *attractive* and will never be fat. You want to live for all those beautiful things God has for you, yourself, your family, boyfriends and most important children, little people you can bring into this beautiful world, yes, it is beautiful even I say that. All the lovely places, the sand, sea and countryside, trees, flowers, birds, you can give them all that you missed in your childhood.

You have a kind nature, I can just see what a wonderful mother you will make.

Help other anorectics, write a book. You are good at drawing,

paint what it feels like. Remember *only you can* and WILL
OVERCOME IT.

Patricia, my mother you can always talk to her at anytime.
There was never a time when I didn't tell her something about
me. She will help you and will honestly seem like me. She has
said I must tell you this. She can help pull and talk you through
it.

I must go, I'm tired.
    All my love,
        Catherine.

From hospital Patricia wrote to a friend,

When she died it was really sad. I went up to see her mum
and I knew something was wrong because I had tried phoning
all day and it was engaged, and when I went up to the house
her bedroom light was off. Her mum answered the door and I
knew straight away. I stayed in Catherine's mum's arms and
she explained everything to me, most of all that Catherine was
at peace now, rid of the devil that lived inside her. It gave me
strength, it made me want to kill the devil in me even more
because it killed the best friend I could ever have.

It was on the fourteenth of December that Anna returned
home from medical school; she had visited regularly at
weekends throughout the term and each time had become
more distressed on witnessing Catherine's deterioration.
Catherine was now totally bedridden, incontinent and
unable to do anything for herself. Anna became my second
pair of hands, my other pair of feet. The gentleness,
compassion, patience and love she gave Catherine was
limitless. Simon and Jenny, now both qualified and working,
would come whenever they could. They both cared for
Catherine the day I went out to do my Christmas shopping.
On my return, Catherine told me how well they had looked
after her.

'Only Jenny can make my blackcurrant drink the way I

like it!' she added. Richard too would come whenever possible, and nothing gave Catherine greater pleasure than to have the entire family at home. Christmas was now the time she was looking forward to with childlike eagerness.

Catherine had an earnest desire to attend Midnight Mass. In her weakened and fragile condition this simply was not possible. She spoke of her wish to Father John, and he related to her the charming story of St Clare of Assisi.

St Clare, born in the twelfth century, became the foundress of the religious order known as the Poor Clares. One Christmas, lying critically ill in her small cell, she felt an overwhelming longing to attend Midnight Mass and to her great joy she received a miraculous vision of the entire Mass on her cell wall. (Today St Clare is the patron saint of television.)

Catherine found comfort and pleasure in this little story and so, while the family attended our parish church on Christmas Eve, Catherine and I watched the ITV televising of Midnight Mass from Newcastle.

Despite the sadness in all our hearts we attempted to make this Christmas a truly happy one for Catherine. We placed a bed in the drawing-room so that she would be in the midst of all the activity. When it was time for dinner, John, Simon and Richard carried her, bed and all, into the dining-room. There she insisted on me giving her a normal portion of turkey, vegetables and trimmings. She attempted to chew the food but then deposited it in a basin. By now, even chewing food, except for her fruit, made her feel sick, but she was determined on this occasion to share in the festivities as much as she was able. That night when I had settled her comfortably, she said, 'This has been such a lovely day, thank everyone for me for making it so happy.'

The week following Christmas was one of quiet despair for all of us. Catherine was so loving, so giving, but knowing she wanted to die was something we could not come to terms with. We knew her death was inevitable, yet we did not want to believe that she would not pull through as she had done before. Mentally she was incredibly alert and lucid; this I believe made it harder for us to accept; it was like living a nightmare, a nightmare I desperately hoped to wake up from and discover that none of it was real.

Marie travelled from Oxford to see Catherine; she had intended to return the same day but, on John's insistence, stayed the night. Catherine was so pleased. 'It's like a bonus, Mummy. Sister Marie and I will be able to pray tonight and tomorrow morning as well.'

Marie describes how she went to Catherine's room that afternoon.

After sitting in silence for some time Catherine started, 'I wish God would give us a sign.' (She meant a sign about whether she was to live or die.) I replied that the best signs came from our own hearts because our hearts are so deep within us that they are united to God. So, if she could find out what her heart was saying, that would be her sign. Very earnestly, Catherine replied: 'I want to be at peace, in the arms of Jesus, looking down on my family and able to protect them. I want it with all my heart.'

I answered: 'Well then, if your heart wants it, it must be right.'

'You *do* believe me, don't you?'

'I do believe *in* you. And I believe that every person is a mystery, and no one can completely understand anyone else.' I was being confronted with a person whom I could say a total 'Yes' to, yet who went clean contrary to my ideas and instincts. I could not understand. But I can't understand God either.

When Marie left, I sensed an even greater peace in Catherine. She had been so impatient to die, but now she seemed to have grasped that peace and happiness in Jesus are possible on this side of the grave. In the few days she had left she never once asked 'Why hasn't God taken me?' or 'How long do you think it will be before I die?'

Every Sunday for the past two years, the congregation of our church had been asked to pray for Catherine. It seemed like sheer chance that on 1 January I should have been the reader at Mass, but I do not believe it was mere coincidence that I was the one to ask for prayers for Catherine for the last time, nor do I believe it was coincidence that the second reading for that Mass happened to be the very prayer that my sister Eileen was saying as Catherine drew her last breath.

May the Lord bless you and keep you
May his face shine on you and be gracious to you
May the Lord uncover his face to you and give you his peace.
                                                    Numbers, 6.

Later that day I became more concerned for Catherine. Her pain had intensified. I telephoned Dr Foot who advised me to increase the dosage of Brompton mixture which she had prescribed for Catherine for the previous two days. Sitting with Catherine, I asked 'Would you like to be anointed?' She nodded her head. Feeling frantic and threatened, I left her bedside and made what must have been an incoherent call to Father Taggart, our parish priest. He came immediately.

I slept in Catherine's room that night, getting into the camp bed which had been placed beside her. She said 'My Mummy and me sleeping in the same room, how lovely.' Feeling utterly exhausted, but relieved to be lying down at last, I heard her ask 'Is my room tidy?' Richard put his head round the door to say goodnight, and he added, 'Don't you two stay awake all night gossiping!'

Catherine slept for six hours, the best night she had had for many weeks. When she awoke she looked at me, her little face radiant. She said, 'I am so happy, God is with me.' These were her last clear words.

At about two-thirty in the afternoon, Catherine indicated that she would like to be bathed. Anna helped me.

Mummy and I carried her to the bathroom and while I supported her in the bath, mummy washed her. At one point I changed the way I was holding her and her head hit the side of the bath; I was concerned in case she was hurt, and when asked if she was all right she just nodded. She gave the impression that she did not know she was in the bath or perhaps could not see what was going on round her. I think now I look back that she may have been blind and did not realize the fact, or else did not want to let us know she could no longer see. Mummy went downstairs to answer the front door, while I talced Catherine as she lay on towels on the bathroom floor. All she mouthed was, 'Loads, loads,' as I put the talcum powder on her. I wanted to make her smell lovely and feel refreshed. I wanted to show her how much I cared. Mummy and I then dressed her in a brand-new nightie. I told her how pretty she looked as I brushed her hair; I really loved her and wanted to show it.

That last day of Catherine's life I sensed that her time here on earth was almost up, yet I couldn't and wouldn't allow myself to believe it. She was so sharp, so lucid, I wanted her for myself. At lunchtime my sister Eileen telephoned me to ask if she and two of her daughters could come to visit Catherine. I told her no, but then my mother came on the phone and said how much she wanted to see her, and I couldn't refuse her. When they arrived the stillness and tranquillity of the house contrasted vividly with the driving rain and gale-force winds outside. Catherine was sleeping so deeply and peacefully, the candlelight giving an added softness to her pale skin and a lustre to her dark hair. Later that evening her spirit soared and she was finally released from all her pain and suffering.

Catherine died at 6.55 p.m. on 2 January 1984. She died at peace with God, with herself, with us, and with a heart full of love.

THE FATHER'S STORY
John Dunbar

For me a secure home, marriage and family always meant a great deal. It was important in my view that I dedicated myself completely to achieving financial independence for myself and the family, leaving the home and the children entirely in my wife's capable hands. This did not mean that I ignored the children. It meant that when they were babies I did not have time or interest to share the changing, feeding, bathing and other tasks. When they grew out of this stage, however, I always took a great interest in their schooling, taught them games, and tried never to miss special school days when parents were invited, or they were performing or playing matches.

It was my belief that the husband should control and take full responsibility for all family money matters and that the children should be brought up to obey. Discipline was perhaps strict, and my style was termed 'Victorian'.

I was delighted when our first baby was a boy, but after two boys it was a great delight for us all when our first girl, Catherine, was born. My memories of Catherine's early years are of a very obstinate and strong-willed little girl. In a way, there was somehow a battle of wills between Catherine and myself. She used to play on this by teasing me with her attention; she used to say: 'Daddy, I'm goin(g) to le(t) you pu(t) me to bed tonigh(t)' (dropping the ends of her words due to a speech difficulty). Then when bedtime came she would say: 'Daddy, I change(d) my mind, not goin(g) to le(t) you pu(t) me to bed tonigh(t).'

As Catherine grew older it was a pleasure to see her play with her little sister, Anna, and to enjoy the love and happiness which the four children gave to us and to each other.

We often went out to eat as a family, and here Catherine was always tremendously fussy as to what she chose from her limited range of favourite foods and how it was cooked. Tomato soup, followed by egg and chips was a special favourite, but the egg and chips would be sent back if the egg was underdone or the chips insufficiently browned.

My early years were spent with my grandparents in Liverpool, at a time of food scarcity during the war; and our diet was further limited because of shortage of money. I was brought up on the discipline that if you couldn't eat something you didn't put it on your plate. If you did take it, however, you must eat every scrap. Common sayings were 'Waste not, want not,' and 'Always get up from the table wanting more.' I applied the same discipline to my children, expecting them to eat everything on their plates and insisting that they did so. Catherine's fussiness, particularly in restaurants, was a constant annoyance to me. Once, when passing through Madrid, I gave the family a special treat by taking them to lunch at Botins, one of the oldest and best restaurants in the old town, near the Plaza Mayor. The specialities – *angulas bilbaínas* (sizzling hot little eels no thicker than spaghetti served with garlic) followed by roast suckling pig – were selected by all except Catherine. She ordered fried eggs and chips, but unfortunately the eggs were underdone and had to be returned to the kitchen twice. This made me furious.

Looking back at these early years before Catherine's anorexia started, I feel that my upbringing regarding food, and the way I applied it to my children, may have been a contributing factor to Catherine's later eating problems. I only wish now that I had ignored what she ate and let her leave what she wished. Also, that I had hidden my annoyance at her fussiness and let her enjoy meals in her own way.

All the children strove to achieve something in their sport and studies. They all attended a convent kindergarten, and then went on to preparatory school, followed by public school. There was never any pressure on them to pass exams; I constantly reminded them that I was paying for this expensive education to make them grow up better people, not to collect O levels and A levels. In my view, Catherine had average intelligence, but she worked so hard that she was always at the top end of her year. She was exceptionally talented at drama, good at ballet, and had a beautiful singing voice. We purchased guitars in Spain for the two girls and they took lessons and sang together. Catherine also was good at sport, gymnastics, tennis and swimming – in fact, everything she tackled she did well. She also was a recognized leader, being appointed as prefect and head girl not only by her teachers, but also by the votes of her classmates.

As parents we always watched Catherine in school plays and in poetry festivals, where she was one of the best and sometimes took top prizes. On one occasion, at the age of eleven, on the boat coming home from Spain, she entered a children's competition and won with her recitation of 'The Raggle-taggle Gypsies'.

As a father, I took great delight in seeing my two daughters grow up as attractive, vivacious and exceptionally pretty girls. I remember attending a gymnastic and ballet display at Catherine's school when she was nearly fourteen, and feeling so proud. She had a beautiful face, lovely long hair and a delightful trim, athletic figure. Catherine never showed signs of excess weight and it was a subject which never came up for discussion in regard to the children. My wife and myself, however, have had to fight against weight problems all our lives, and this was a subject on which Dad was often teased, but never Mum.

Up to December 1973 we appeared to be an ideal family, in love with each other, no favourites, the boys and the girls being happy companions to each other. Financially we were moving ahead rapidly; I had an excellent career with a good income and benefits. We had a large Victorian house of immense character, where we had lived for eleven years. In addition, we had family property, investments and a major shareholding in a small private group of industrial companies which I had built up.

Perhaps we were too stable and boredom crept in, in any case, one day I decided we should look at houses further out in the country with land, tennis courts, swimming-pool, etc. We found an idyllic house with all these amenities about fifteen minutes' drive from our existing home. We made an offer but withdrew it after survey. It was then auctioned while I was abroad and my wife bid to our limit, but was beaten. The family had become so excited that there were some tears, and I personally felt a great sense of failure. It was the first time my family really wanted something and I had not been able to provide it.

The unusual then happened. The sale fell through and we were offered the house again. As we had not sold our existing house it meant heavy bridging finance and an element of risk, but property had been going through a tremendous boom and all our professional advisers said: 'You have always made decisions for business reasons, go ahead and make this for the family – you can't lose much.'

It was an emotional rather than a logical decision, and the results of that one decision brought us near bankruptcy, tore our family to shreds, and, I believe, was the main factor in Catherine 'protesting' through giving up eating – the easiest way for her, as she had never been a great eater.

A few months after we purchased the new house the world economy collapsed, property prices tumbled and interest rates rose, and we had to live with huge debts covered by assets which were unsaleable, and with ever-increasing borrowings to cover interest that could not be paid. My job became very precarious as the European investment group by whom I was retained had a number of investment disasters in Europe, and they decided to sell off the remainder and close the company. The private group of companies which I had built up also suffered, and strains amongst the major shareholders combined with the bad economic situation destroyed their profitability one by one.

We held on to the country home for three years, but eventually had to sell, as I was losing my income and most of my investments; selling at a loss became the only method of survival. One day Catherine was playing tennis with me as Maureen was showing prospective purchasers around the grounds. Catherine stopped playing, came up to the net, stamped her foot and said: 'Daddy, why are these people looking at our house? Why don't they go away?' She knew we were selling but it seemed to hit her suddenly when she saw the viewers that day.

From early 1974 onwards life became a nightmare of fear, depression and fighting for survival like a caged animal. I was determined to keep the children at their existing schools, and unfortunately they all reached public-school age during the first few years of the crisis. In addition, just before we sold the house, Catherine begged me to let her be a boarder; despite the extra financial burden I agreed, to keep her happy.

My personal survival crisis and my behaviour during this period had a very severe effect on the family, particularly on Maureen and Catherine – the boys were away at school and Anna was probably too young. I felt that the family did not appreciate that every moment of my life I was facing more and larger financial shocks, and that I was determined we would survive at any cost. Frequently, the strain, the sense of failure, the fear of the future, and the fight to pay bills became too much for me. As an ex-drinking Rugby man, I used to decide sometimes to drink myself into oblivion, or I tried to recuperate by taking my depression to bed for a weekend. Each of these methods seemed to get me back into fighting mood again and without this I would never have survived personally or financially.

The effect on my family was very great; there were outbursts because of money, outbursts because I felt deserted and unappreciated by my family in my crisis. Many times Catherine with her determination and strong will clashed with me.

We sold the house and within a year had sold another property. We moved into a flat in central London which had belonged to one of my companies and had two years remaining on the lease. Almost everything else had been lost and my job was moving to an end.

Catherine started to have digestive problems before we moved to central London, and then stopped eating altogether after we had moved.

I had now eliminated my debts but had lost almost all my assets and investments, and in a few months would be losing my salary. So now it was a fight to get a job.

When Catherine stopped eating, my immediate reaction

was to force her to sit at the table until she did so. Her violent reactions and uncharacteristic verbal abuse of her parents was absolutely staggering. I then tried to offer rewards to induce her and tried to think of ways to break the pattern which was setting in. It was obvious that only her mother could reach Catherine emotionally, and therefore my role was again organizing and providing. In the first years of her treatment, I never faced or believed that this beautiful daughter would eventually die of anorexia some seven years later.

Unfortunately, during those seven years I was still fighting to survive and sort out some future from the tangled ends of our financial disasters.

My first consideration was my future employment, and I decided to accept a very attractive appointment in the Middle East rather than the alternative of uprooting the family from schools, etc., and emigrating to an equally attractive opportunity in Australia.

Catherine went into hospital, had frequent psychiatric treatment and even went to school in France for a term to try and break the pattern of her habits. We drove her to France before I left for the Middle East, and she came home at half term, just before I was due to take up my new appointment. She seemed happy and in good health. When I took her to the airport to make her return for the second half of term she was a little uncertain. After being in Saudi Arabia for only a few weeks, I learnt that Catherine's condition had again become serious.

Before going to Saudi Arabia I had, in my usual manner, laid down the specifications and amenities which I wanted for a new house, as the lease in central London was expiring within a year. Catherine badly wanted a house with a garden, which would have been simple, but I insisted on a country house of character. After almost a year of viewing, my wife found a house in Wiltshire and proceeded to modernize it from top to bottom. Unfortunately, Catherine's illness was a reason for keeping my wife in the UK, apart from three visits of a month to Saudi, and for me this meant an added strain in a strange and hostile land.

The house in Wiltshire was a disaster – far away from friends and relatives and too far for the children to visit frequently at weekends. From the moment I saw it I was filled with doom and foreboding.

During my two years in Saudi Arabia I visited home frequently, but Catherine and I grew farther apart. On the one hand Catherine saw her life with her mother as a haven of security in which she could live as an anorectic, and on the other she was fearful of my return because of the years of family trouble she had experienced from 1973. While I was abroad, life probably appeared calm with her mother. The money flowed in to keep everyone at a good standard of living and to maintain Catherine at secretarial college.

Catherine still knew how to play on my emotions however. Once, when I returned to the UK just before Christmas, my wife and I visited the psychiatrist in the hospital where Catherine was having treatment as an inpatient. Everyone decided to keep the visit secret from Catherine until after our consultation. Somehow, however, Catherine found out, and was waiting at the top of the elevator. She threw her arms around me, crying: 'Daddy, Daddy, take me home for Christmas.' I did, even though the hospital felt she should stay. Maybe I was wrong, but how could we have enjoyed a family Christmas with Catherine miles away in hospital?

Towards the end of my period abroad Catherine became hostile to my visits. Eventually, on one occasion when I arrived unexpectedly, she refused to eat until I packed and went to stay with a friend. What else could I do? She was protecting the life that she had built up with her mother – I was a threat.

Eventually I abandoned Saudi Arabia, which had become a nightmare life for me. After a few uneasy weeks at home Maureen decided she needed to go away and didn't return again permanently for some months. During this period Catherine became a tower of strength. She did all the housekeeping and cooking, gave me encouragement in my depression, and made me try to build back to normality. In other words, she took over the role of wife, and also mother to her younger sister, Anna, who was at boarding-school.

There was, however, no letting up in her anorexia; she ruled the kitchen and she screamed if I entered it during her meals. She served my meals in another room. Her drive and determination were incredible. Every day I was forced to take her out on driving practice until she passed her test. Immediately after she passed she was searching everywhere to find a second-hand car and within a week she had persuaded me to buy one for her.

Eventually, it was Catherine who helped me with the move, to a house which needed renovating, refitting and remodelling from top to bottom. We lived together in chaos for some four months. There wasn't one completed room; there were several different contractors working – often three or four at one time. Catherine coped and also took temporary work as a secretary.

Finally Maureen returned and we took a holiday with the two girls. On our return Catherine went back to complete her secretarial-college course and then took a permanent job.

By September 1981 Catherine was becoming weaker again, so I tried sending her with her mother to Venice and Florence for a holiday. There was no positive result from this and by early 1982 she agreed to go into a private hospital. This produced no results and we eventually brought her home some six months later in a weaker condition than when she entered.

Maureen succeeded in improving Catherine's physical state over the next few months. There was, however, little relief from anorectic behaviour. Eventually, to save my younger daughter from the immense strain during her A levels, I legally committed Catherine to a private hospital in a last desperate attempt to save her life. She was forced to put on weight. When she came out, she took a job until physically she could no longer travel to London.

Her determination was evidenced when she drove us both to the station on the last day she was able to work. She was obsessed with catching her normal train. It arrived as she was at the bottom of a flight of twenty steps up to the platform. She could hardly put one foot in front of the other. I held up the train, and she eventually climbed in – I knew it was to be her last day at work. The company sent her home.

It had been nearly four years since I had returned home. We had all suffered much, and now faced the inevitable – Catherine wanted to die, and without a miracle I was resigned to the fact that she would die.

I tried as best I could to behave normally, but sometimes I showed my irritation at Catherine's demands. She was, however, always understanding and patient. One thing that irritated me, and had done for a long time, was her smoking. Since a child I have hated the smell and the sight of smoking, and it is a great source of personal strain that some of my family smoke. It was especially difficult to live with during Catherine's last few months. First, I hated the habit, and secondly it was impossible for me to rationalize a girl who could not eat but could smoke. Why, oh why, couldn't she eat instead of smoke? I now know the logic: anorectics smoke because their craving requires something constantly in their mouth.

In my view, no one or no one event was totally to blame for Catherine's illness. It was the effect of her own physical and mental make-up combined with the traumas and stresses of the family and the interaction of the individuals in it. Catherine was given every possible medical treatment and all the help and love which we could summon up during our years of family crisis.

Looking back I remember my strictness with the children, which probably made them nervous of me. I think of my depressions and rages during our family problems, which surely affected them deeply. I remember my lack of understanding that such a logical intelligent girl could do this to herself; my sheer anger, intolerance and frustration, which I used to often voice to her in an effort to shake her off this fatal course. I tried logic, bribery, threats and pleading with her, even though it upset her. I had to keep on trying in the hope that any change of emotion might arouse her desire and will to fight to live.

All that I did or said was the best I could do at that time in those circumstances. My logical mind could not comprehend, but sadly there is no logic in anorexia. There will always be a deep feeling of extreme failure, sorrow and pain for the loss of a lovely daughter with an illness which no one fully understands. I loved her dearly.

AFTERWORD
Simon Dunbar

As a young and newly qualified doctor I don't expect everyone to agree with my analysis of anorexia nervosa. However, having seen my sister suffer and eventually die of this disease has, I believe, given me an insight which others may not possess.

My relationship with Catherine was very much that of a brother to a younger sister. Yet, strangely, I would sometimes feel she was years older and almost a mother to me. Despite the manipulative ways and awkwardness created by her illness, even though she would sometimes say how she hated us and didn't trust us, we knew with certainty that deep down she loved and needed us. This loving side of her character became strongly evident in the last months of her life, when she became more at peace with herself and felt that she had brought us to an understanding of her situation.

Anorexia nervosa generally begins in and around puberty, affecting females more commonly than males. It is not, as the unfortunate cliché would have it, a 'slimmers' disease', a phrase which represents an insensitive misunderstanding of the syndrome, which does not occur as a direct result of slimming or dieting. Furthermore, it gives the impression of an illness which is self-induced and easily reversible, although nothing could be further from the truth. The anorectic is full of hatred which is directed at herself and her illness. The latter gives her a sense of control and security, and the fear of losing this is so great that, despite all the anguish, suffering and inward struggles which are present, she is trapped. Incorrect management and treatment increase her fears and force her to retreat further into the security of her illness. The anorexia therefore gains greater control and the prognosis becomes worse.

A precise definition of anorexia nervosa is difficult because of the complexity and diversity of each individual case – the cause is deep-rooted in the psyche of the individual and her relationship with her family and her environment – but in general terms it can be described as a syndrome which manifests itself as LOSS OF BODY WEIGHT, LOSS OF BODY SHAPE and CESSATION OF MENSTRUATION. This triad is the result of reduced food intake and failure to make the transition from puberty to womanhood. Other features of the syndrome which may be present are as follows:

1. Calorie counting.
2. Encouraging others to eat.
3. Increased interest in what others eat.
4. Increased interest in cooking and food.
5. Hoarding food.
6. Shoplifting (often food).
7. Daily weighing.
8. Preoccupation with body weight and shape.
9. Wearing baggy clothes (to hide body shape).
10. Binging and vomiting.
11. Laxative abuse.
12. Overactivity and increased mental alertness.
13. Tendency to be manipulative.
14. Obsessive and ritualistic behaviour.
15. Depression and withdrawal.

16. Anxiety and panic attacks.
17. Low self-esteem.
18. Self-hatred.
19. Suicide attempts.
20. Other effects of malnutrition.

Anorexia nervosa represents an arrest of puberty and, in severe cases, a reversion towards childhood, something which becomes reflected in the physical and mental appearance and attitude of the individual. She gains satisfaction and security from the way in which she is able to suppress her hunger and control her body weight and shape. She stops or fails to menstruate and loses or does not develop her female body form. Eventually, it is the anorexia which gains control and becomes an integral part of her personality from which it is increasingly difficult to escape. Food, body shape and weight become an obsession. Life is built around a strict routine and people and situations are manipulated to ensure this is not broken. Eventually, her concept of her own body becomes completely distorted and she genuinely feels she is fat and bloated. Ironically, the anorectic is continually hungry and craves food, and this and other conflicts take their toll both physically and mentally. Hence low self-esteem, anxiety, depression and even attempted suicide add themselves to the picture. Her life becomes so vastly different from ours that she withdraws and becomes increasingly unable to take part in normal life.

In my opinion, all cases of anorexia nervosa are brought about by great emotional upset, trauma or sadness. This may be caused by something acute, but more often is the result of ongoing environmental or family circumstances which are of immense importance to the individual concerned, so much so that their existence creates enormous mental turmoil and upheaval, leading to a destruction of confidence and craving for stability and security. Puberty is in any case a time of imbalance, when mental and physical adjustments are being made as adolescence proceeds to adulthood, and susceptible individuals are at their most vulnerable. (These girls are often intelligent and highly sensitive.)

The correct treatment of anorexia nervosa is crucial because mistakes can so easily precipitate the illness in the wrong direction. Setbacks strengthen the anorectic's resolve and increase the grip which the illness has on her. It is important to grasp that the anorectic has an enormous fear of recovery. To apply force only increases this, causing her to withdraw further into the security given by her illness. It is of the greatest importance, therefore, to gain her confidence and trust first of all. The basis of treatment is a contract, and for this to be effective it must be entered into voluntarily by both parties. The only role that sectioning (committing someone to hospital under the Mental Health Act) has to play is to initiate medical treatment in a life-threatening situation. The treatment of the anorexia must be kept completely separate so that trust and confidence are not destroyed.

The basis of treatment must be to take the young girl through the puberty that she has never had, to teach her what she would otherwise have learned naturally. In this way she will be able to gain the control and security she requires in life from womanhood and from what is around her, rather than from her illness. All aspects of the illness have to be tackled. She must relearn how to eat, dress, and develop relationships, and many other things. Ideally, and in severe cases particularly, this should be carried out by a specialist team in a specialized unit, able to provide twenty-four-hour support and therapy. The treatment of problems connected with food, weight and eating should be blended in with the rest of the programme and as little fuss made about them as possible – nothing is worse than to confront an anorectic with mountains of food and set her a target weight which she finds daunting and unattainable. Helping her to make plans for the future and rebuilding her self-esteem and confidence are just as important. Because of the nature of the condition it is essential to determine its underlying cause and attempt to deal with it. This will necessarily mean involving the whole family at various stages during treatment, as there is often some underlying family pathology and, at the very least, their understanding and support can be invaluable. There is absolutely no point in treating an anorectic only to place her back in the environment where the illness was created, thus placing her at risk once again.

Many cases of anorexia resolve themselves in the early stages. It is, however, important to be aware of the dangers and to know that one must seek help early, before the anorexia gains control.